SILENT MOVIES

SILENT MOVIES

NEIL SINYARD

GALLERY BOOKS
An imprint of W.H. Smith Publishers Inc.
112 Madison Avenue
New York, New York 10016

PAGE 2
TOP: *Son of the Sheik:*
Rudolph Valentino and
Vilma Banky.
MIDDLE: *Ben-Hur:* Ramon
Novarro and May McAvoy.
BOTTOM: Abel Gance's
Napoleon.

THIS PAGE
RIGHT: Abel Gance (second
from right) directs
Napoleon.
BELOW: Cecil B DeMille
(right) at work in the 1920s.

Published by Gallery Books
A Division of W H Smith Publishers Inc.
112 Madison Avenue
New York, New York 10016

Produced by
Brompton Books Corp.
15 Sherwood Place
Greenwich, CT 06830

Copyright © 1990 Brompton Books Corp.

ISBN 0-8317-7800-8

Printed in Hong Kong

10 9 8 7 6 5 4 3 2 1

Contents

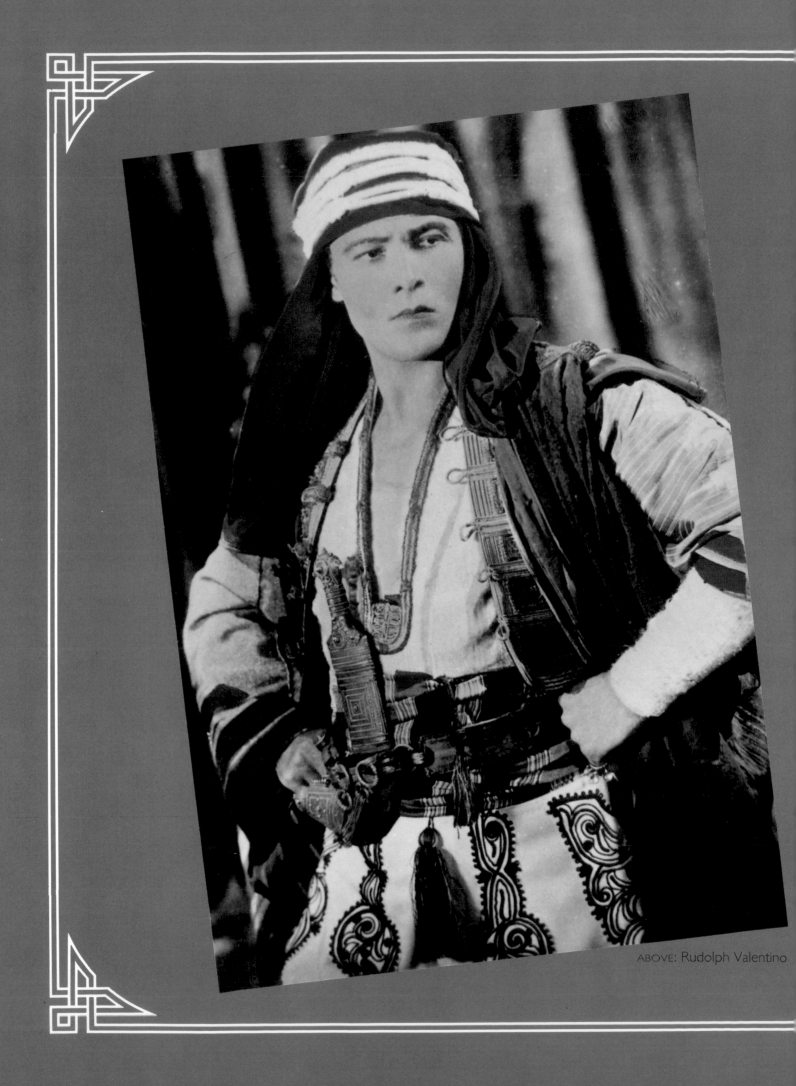

ABOVE: Rudolph Valentino

CHAPTER ONE
White Magic

———

'Still wonderful, isn't it?' says the ex-movie queen of the silent era (Gloria Swanson), as she watches one of her old movies in Billy Wilder's SUNSET BOULEVARD (1950). 'And no dialogue,' she adds meaningfully to her companion (William Holden), who is a screenwriter of the new Hollywood. 'We didn't need dialogue — we had faces.'

Many film fans and historians even today would concur with the implicit view of Gloria Swanson's movie heroine: namely, that the silent era was the cinema's Golden Age, a period of unrivaled innovation, experiment and excitement that was in essence unrepeatable and has never been surpassed. In a mere three decades the cinema leapt from being a crude technological curiosity, to a new universal language, a mass entertainment industry and the art form of the twentieth century.

Silent cinema is constantly being rediscovered. In some cases, the rediscovery has been literal: a French classic, Raymond Bernard's MIRACLE OF THE WOLVES, believed lost, turning up in a flea market; the original version of Carl Dreyer's classic THE PASSION OF JOAN OF ARC being found in 1985 in an asylum in Norway; and 'blue movies' of the 1890s recently being unearthed and offering some revealing documentary footage on Victorian lingerie. In other cases rediscovery has taken the form of a reminder. Forty years ago, in a famous essay entitled 'Comedy's Greatest Era' in *Life* magazine, James Agee wrote so evocatively of the greatness of silent film comedy that he provoked nostalgia among his older readers who remembered those times, and envy among the younger who had not seen them. The essay is generally regarded as having given a considerable fillip to the ailing career at that time of Buster Keaton. In the 1950s and 1960s, the advent of television and the production of some skillful compilation films brought the manic marvels of the Keystone Kops, Harold Lloyd and Laurel and Hardy to a new generation of film fans. More recently, a silent classic like Fritz Lang's METROPOLIS has taken on a new lease of life, both as a West End musical and in a re-edited film version with a new score by Giorgio Moroder.

However, if rediscovery means restoration, undoubtedly the most significant event of the last decade towards the reevaluation of silent cinema has been the spectacular presentation of Abel Gance's NAPOLEON. It was shown in London in 1980 after painstaking restoration work by the film historian Kevin Brownlow and with a new score by Carl Davis; and later in America with a score by Carmine Coppola. Restored to its full length with its imaginative use of color and innovative use of wide screen also on display, this epic of cinematic imagination could be appreciated afresh. For director Francis Ford Coppola, it demonstrated that silent films could make money and indeed might even change people's ideas of the way films are made and shown. There has been no evidence of this as yet, but the success of NAPOLEON undoubtedly facilitated the proper showings, with new scores, of other silent masterpieces such as D W Griffith's BROKEN BLOSSOMS, Victor Sjöström's THE WIND, King Vidor's THE CROWD and the Kozintsev-Trauberg classic of Soviet silent cinema, NEW BABYLON, with music by the young Dmitri Shostakovich. In 1986, to commemorate the 70th anniversary of D W Griffith's INTOLERANCE, those superb film composers of the modern French cinema, Pierre Jansen and Antoine Duhamel were commissioned to write a new score to accompany the presentation of the film. It is hard to imagine that this would have been possible without the prior success of NAPOLEON.

There has been more to the restoration of NAPOLEON than simply the opportunity of showing a great film to a new audience. It was also an attempt to put the record straight. Previously the film had only been viewable in an abbreviated, mutilated form. The new presentation at least allowed the film to be shown in a form that the director himself would have approved. Behind all this was a more general polemical intent: to rescue the reputation of silent movies from the status of being regarded by the postwar generation of filmgoers as primitive, jerky, monochrome relics. If you restore them to the condition in which they were originally seen, an audience can recognize that many were fully scored, atmospherically tinted and quite beautifully photographed. Also, far from being primitive, silent films had a power that was to have a profound influence on the directors of the sound era. Fred Zinnemann, award-winning director of such classics as HIGH NOON (1952) and FROM HERE TO ETERNITY (1953), said his ambition to become a film maker came basically from the impact on him of three films: King Vidor's THE BIG PARADE, Sergei Eisenstein's BATTLESHIP POTEMKIN and Carl Dreyer's JOAN OF ARC. The idiosyncratic director of AGUIRRE – WRATH OF GOD (1973) and FITZCARRALDO (1982), Werner Herzog, has commented that the new German cinema has no fathers, only grandfathers – referring to the legacy of such masters of the German silent cinema as Fritz Lang and F W Murnau.

Perhaps it should be stressed at this stage that the term 'silent movies' was always something of a misnomer. For one thing they were never shown in silence. First-run films often had a full symphonic score to accompany the action and even the local nickelodeon had its resident pianist. One of André Previn's earliest musical memories is playing the piano as a boy during the 1930s in a cinema showing old silent films. He was to be undone by the cross cutting in D W Griffith's INTOLERANCE. ('At one point, I thought they had settled into a nice long sequence of Charleston-dancing flappers and I swung whole-heartedly into *Tiger Rag*. The next thing I saw was the manager, apoplectic, storming down the center aisle – I'd not noticed that Griffith had cut back to the Crucifixion'.) It should also be remembered that for people in those days there was no such thing as a 'silent movie' – they were just movies. Dialogue was not missed any more than a vocal score would be missed from a symphony. It was just not part of the new medium's language. Gloria Swanson never lost her distaste for the phrase: 'Critics seemed astonished', she said in her autobiography, 'when I informed them I found talking pictures no more difficult to make than – I recoiled as I heard myself using their phrase – silent pictures'.

Film historians increasingly appreciate that silent film was not a crude, incomplete form of sound film but essentially a different medium – as different, says historian William K Everson, as painting from sculpture. Recent research and projection practice have removed a lot of misconceptions. If silent movies often seemed jerky or too fast, it was not due to technical incompetence: it was simply that, on modern machines, they were being projected at the wrong speed. The growth in film studies in schools, colleges and universities over the last two decades has seen a corresponding interest in and reevaluation of film history. This has involved a closer look at that early period which saw the evolution of film language – the close up, the dissolve, rapid cutting etc. – and the development of the film industry – the star system, the studios, cinema chains, the growth of Hollywood – that nowadays we take for granted. It has also involved a reevaluation of standard practices of silent cinema that have either been taken for granted or even derided. For example, it is now accepted that intertitles, which have often been regarded simply as verbal speech that we cannot hear because of limitations of technology, were deployed by different directors in highly individual ways. In the films of D W Griffith, the titles were almost as idiosyncratic and as personal as the visuals, being full of Biblical quotations, symbolism, moralizing, and emphatic emotional coloration ('Dying, she gives her last smile to a world that has been so unkind', says the title for the heart-rending death of the heroine in BROKEN BLOSSOMS). Conversely the titles in the films of Eisenstein tend to be dynamic, peremptory and abrupt. 'Suddenly. . .' is all that he says to herald one of the most dramatic moments in all cinema: the ominous appearance of the Cossacks on the Odessa steps in BATTLESHIP POTEMKIN (1925), which gives rise to what is still one of the greatest set pieces in film history.

Who would have thought that so advanced an example of cinematic syntax as Eisenstein's 'Odessa steps' sequence could have been created only 30 years after the event that signaled the 'invention' of

RIGHT: Louis Lumière, a pioneer of moving pictures who invented a cine camera in 1893.

BELOW: Massacre on the Odessa Steps in *Battleship Potemkin*.

CINÉMATOGRAPHE LUMIÈRE

LEFT: Early poster for Lumière Cinématographe, with the audience watching 'Watering the Gardener'.

BELOW LEFT: Albert Dieudonné as Napoleon.

BELOW: Thomas Edison, whom Einstein described as 'the greatest inventor of all time'.

BOTTOM RIGHT: Eadward Muybridge's early photographic record of 'animal locomotion'.

the cinema? Certainly not Louis and Auguste Lumière who, in December 1895, organized what is generally regarded as the first truly public performance of motion pictures at the Grand Café, Boulevard des Capucines, Paris. The event was really the culmination of numerous photographic developments that had taken place over the preceding decades. These included Eadweard Muybridge's famous photographs of horses in motion in 1871; Etienne Jules Marey's development of a so called 'photographic rifle' with which he could take ten pictures a second (the term 'shooting' for a film is commonly thought to derive from this); George Eastman's launch in 1888 of the Kodak camera ('you press the button, we do the rest,' was the famous slogan) and his development of the celluloid roll film; and Thomas Edison's production in 1891 of 35mm film and, with his brilliant assistant W K L

Dickson, the development of the Kinetograph and the Kinetoscope which showed photographic moving pictures in a peepshow. The Lumière film show was not only a continuation of all this, but part of a whole era of what has been called 'white magic' – the astonishing technological inventiveness that was to be one of the most striking features of the late nineteenth century. Nevertheless, whether the Lumières understood the significance of the occasion is debatable: 'Our invention can be exploited for a certain time as a scientific curiosity,' said Auguste Lumière, 'but apart from that, it has no commercial future whatsoever.' One of the sad ironies of early film history is that so many of its pioneers – one thinks also of Georges Méliès and Edwin S Porter – either had little business sense or tended to be overtaken by events, with the result that they were forgotten by the industry they helped to found.

What did audiences see at this first film show? They saw films lasting approximately one minute each, intended simply as photographic fragments of human experience, and on the following subjects: Workers Leaving the Lumière factory; Baby at the Breakfast Table; Demolition of a Wall; Watering the Gardener; Congress of Photographic Societies, July 1895; Train Entering a station; A Game of Cards; and A Boat Leaving Harbor. It is probably impossible to imagine nowadays the impact of the occasion. The train's approach to the station is alleged to have caused panic as it moved into close up, as audiences feared the train might come through the screen. 'A Boat Leaving Harbor' was fascinating, not so much

because of the dramatic situation – a boat threatened by waves – but because of the visual experience. For the first time, a backdrop was behaving realistically. Perhaps the most popular sequence was 'Watering the Gardener', in which a man is seen watering the garden, a mischievous boy places his foot on the hose and stops the jet, the gardener looks down the nozzle, at which point the boy releases his foot and the gardener is sprayed with water. This is probably the first silent film comedy, a precursor of the antics of the Mack Sennett Company.

The critical and artistic response to the event was varied and very interesting. Writing in the *New Review* after the British premiere of the Lumière program in 1896, the critic O Winter was unimpressed. The film camera seemed to him a gadget that just reproduced nature 'without selection,' and was mechanical rather than artistic. Dismissively, but very astutely, he compared what the Lumières were doing on film with what Zola was doing in the novel: accumulating external data rather than analyzing the human drama. Conversely, the great Russian writer, Maxim Gorky, after viewing the Lumière program, commented: 'The thirst for such strange fantastic sensations as it gives will grow even greater and we will be increasingly less able and less willing to grasp the everyday impression of life'. For Leo Tolstoy, the cinema's 'swift change of scene, this blending of emotion and experience', was to seem 'much better than the heavy, long-drawn out writing to which we are accustomed. It is closer to life'. For writers of the early twentieth century, the cinema was to represent a considerable stimulus and challenge. At a stroke it

supplanted the novel's supremacy in the art of story-telling and realistic representation.

If Louis Lumière is generally regarded as the father of the realist film and the documentary, the father of fantasy can be said to be Georges Méliès. This generalization needs some modification; as we have seen, Lumière also made comedy, while Méliès made films which reconstructed topical events, such as the trial of Dreyfus, but in broad terms, it is accurate. It is a comparison that has been used ever since to describe the two major tendencies to which the cinema throughout its history has been drawn: film as magic carpet (the Méliès tradition) or film as window on the world (the Lumière tradition). The comparison partially stems from their different backgrounds. Whereas Lumière came to cinema via photography and was therefore understandably drawn towards the reproduction of reality, Méliès came to cinema through the theater, and, more specifically, via magic, for he was a stage magician. He was the first to use artificial light for film making; the first to make commercials; and was an indefatigable technical experimenter, playing around with the possibilities of superimposition, stop action and other film conjuring-tricks. The title of one of his films, VOYAGE ACROSS THE IMPOSSIBLE (1904), gives the clue to the nature of Méliès' cinema. He was a cinematic Jules Verne, making films about fantastic journeys, like his famous A TRIP TO THE MOON in 1902 or his CONQUEST OF THE POLE in 1912, where he plays the part of a professor who participates in a race to the North Pole, pitting his own eccentric flying machine against a car and a balloon. By 1913 his career in the cinema was over and, 16 years later, he was discovered, near destitute, selling toys and sweets in a railway station. In 1953 the great French director, Georges Franju made a short documentary tribute to Méliès, honoring one of the cinema's earliest illusionists.

In the ten years or so after the Lumière screening, Europe was the main sphere of activity for film making. In England R S Paul made a celebrated film of the Derby in 1896, and Cecil Hepworth wrote one of the earliest film books, *The A to Z of Cinematography*, as well as becoming an acclaimed film maker in his own right. Hepworth's RESCUED BY ROVER (1905) not only created the first canine star, but was so popular that the cinemas ran out of prints and Hepworth had to re-shoot it to provide more copies. Meanwhile, in America Thomas Edison is credited with being the

ABOVE: The first canine star of the screen; Cecil Hepworth's *Rescued by Rover*, featuring his family collie as Rover.

LEFT AND RIGHT: Georges Méliès's *Voyage to the Moon*, illustrating the cinema's early capacity for fantasy and imagination.

first man to have a film copyrighted, FRED OTT'S
SNEEZE in 1894, and, in order to accommodate his
camera built a film studio, nicknamed 'The Black
Maria'. However, rather like Lumière and Méliès,
Edison was slow to recognize the commercial
potential of the new medium. The first major step
for American film making was made by an Edison
employee, a cameraman and assistant who was put
in charge of production at Edison's studios, Edwin S
Porter. Porter was to emerge as one of the most interesting figures of early film history, a man whose
work served as a bridge between the so called 'primitive' cinema of the late nineteenth century – where
the camera was primarily simply used as a recorder
of reality – and the new advanced cinema of the
early twentieth century, which saw the development of narrative and where the camera is an instrument that tells the story.

Porter's first important work was THE LIFE OF AN
AMERICAN FIREMAN (1902). (Fire was a burning issue

in the early history of film: one of the earliest major
setbacks had been a Charity Bazaar fire in Paris in
1897, which had claimed the lives of over a hundred
people and whose cause had been traced to a film
machine with the hazardous inflammable nitrate
film.) The British film maker, James Williamson, had
made an acclaimed film on the theme, FIRE, in 1901,
but Porter's film remains the most memorable for
two principal strokes of originality. The first was his
skillful assemblage of early footage to give an impression of a fireman's life and at the same time, to
construct a story film. As Karel Reisz has noted, this
was unprecedented and, importantly, 'implied that
the meaning of a shot was not necessarily self-con-
tained but could be modified by joining the shot to
others'. What we have here are the first stirrings and
recognition of certain properties and characteristics
of film that Sergei Eisenstein would eventually erect
into a theory of montage. The second stroke of
originality was the injection of suspense into an

ostensibly documentary concept, as the film builds to an exciting climax as a mother and her child are rescued from a burning building. The compression of time and the selection of incident for dramatic effect were an early rehearsal and anticipation of the filmic and editing sophistication of D W Griffith, when he came to perfect his famous 'rescued in time' final sequences.

A year later, Porter made the most famous of all early silent films, THE GREAT TRAIN ROBBERY (1903). With film history being in a constant state of flux and new discovery, it is always dangerous to claim a 'first', but certainly in the popular imagination, this film lays claim to being the first western and the first film to tell a story. Also in a chase scene, as the sheriff's posse pursues the robbers, it made innovative use of a moving camera. There was a famous moment where a bandit points a gun directly at the

camera and fires – a moment, exhibitors were told, which could be used either at the opening or the closing of the film.

Porter's career never really lived up to the promise of these early films. The reason for this is simple. He regarded himself as a technician more than a director, an 'artistic engineer' who was left floundering a little when called upon to construct stories and, particularly, to direct actors. He was to make a variety of films, from the social melodrama of the THE EX-CONVICT (1904) to the playful allegory of THE TEDDY BEARS (1907), which was a satire on Theodore Roosevelt in the fantastical mode of Méliès. In THE KLEPTOMANIAC (1906), he made a strong social comment, contrasting the treatment of a wealthy lady for shoplifting (she is let off lightly) with that of a poor mother who is caught stealing bread for her children (she is jailed). In DREAM OF A RAREBIT (1906), his hero, after eating Welsh rarebit, begins to dream about flying over New York; while RESCUED FROM AN EAGLE'S NEST (1907), about a mountaineer who rescues an infant from an eagle, featured a young actor called Lawrence Griffith, who

LEFT: Edwin S Porter directs at the Edison studio in 1908.

BELOW: A thrilling moment from Porter's *The Great Train Robbery.*

was later to change his initials to D W and his profession to director.

Later Porter made something of a specialty of directing leading stage actors in screen adaptations of literary classics. THE COUNT OF MONTE CRISTO (1911), for example, starred James O'Neill, father of playwright Eugene O'Neill. He is probably best remembered today for his son's characterization of him in his play *Long Day's Journey into Night* as a miser who betrayed his talent as an actor in return for financial reward. Stage actors, in the early days of the cinema, did tend to look down on this infant medium, but became gradually more attracted to it, for two overriding reasons: money and immortality. One of the first press reviews of the Lumière showing had immediately drawn attention to this aspect of film: 'With this new invention, death will no longer be absolute, final. The people we have seen on the screen will be with us, moving and alive, after their deaths'. It was this that appealed to actors like James J Hackett, who appeared in THE PRISONER OF ZENDA (1913), and Forbes Robertson whose HAMLET (1914) was preserved on celluloid: film offered the technology to save their theatrical greatness for posterity. As Sarah Bernhardt is alleged to have said to producer Adolph Zukor, who acquired the American distribution rights for her film, QUEEN ELIZABETH (1912): 'Mister Zukor, you have put the best of me in pickle for all time'.

Nevertheless, Porter was sensitive enough to recognize that the future of the cinema lay in more ambitious directions than filmed stage classics, and mild-mannered and modest enough to realize that he lacked the ego to become a major director as the cinema's language grew more sophisticated. 'I can't compete with these new fellers, D W [Griffith] and C B [De Mille]', he told his story editor, B P Schulberg, 'I've had my day'. He returned to the technical sidelines, retiring from the screen and returning to his first love, engineering. He lost his life savings in the Wall Street crash of 1929 and was to die in obscurity in 1941. If Porter remained self-deprecating about his achievement, screenwriter Budd Schulberg (son of B P and future author of *What Makes Sammy Run?* and *On the Waterfront*) was to be more assertive. 'Porter', he said 'opened the door to the art form of the poor'.

Schulberg's comment points to an aspect of early film history to which not enough attention has yet been paid: namely, the response of the audience. Benjamin Hampton has described its early impact in social terms in his book, *A History of the Movies*: 'The telegraph, the telephone, the electric light had created a sensation, but they had not entered into the lives of millions of people. The common man and his family still used kerosene lamps; none but the well-to-do had telephones; and the telegram was a form of communication seldom known in the

RIGHT: The great classical actor, Forbes Robertson in *Hamlet*, directed in 1913 by E Hay Plumb.

LEFT: The legendary Sarah Bernhardt immortalized on celluloid in *Queen Elizabeth*.

average household except to announce serious illness or death. But this new thing – this 'living picture' affair – was not a prosaic tool to reduce labor or to save time; it was not an instrument to create more comfort and luxury for the well to do. It was a romantic device to bring entertainment to the common people'. Film entertainment was cheap (hence the name 'nickelodeons') and offered for the poor and downtrodden substitutes for dreams, images of escape. 'For those whom life has cheated,' said the poet Maravskaya, 'open the electric paradise.' By the time of Porter's retirement from the screen just before the First World War, when there were over 20,000 cinemas in America, a number of smart insiders – producers, directors, actors and actresses – were beginning to sense what an entertainment and industrial gold mine this film business could be. One American director sensed something else: the potential of film as a new art form for the new century. His name was David Wark Griffith.

ABOVE: The noble pro[ofile]
of D W Griffith.

CHAPTER TWO

Poor Man's Shakespeare

'Nothing can take from D W Griffith the wreath
of one of the genuine masters of the American
Cinema.' (Sergei Eisenstein)

Was D W Griffith the greatest director of the silent era, or merely its finest self-publicist? Was he a cinematic innovator, or a throwback to the most traditional form of Victorian melodrama? Since his death in 1948, and indeed some time before then, when his career was in steep decline, Griffith's status as the first film artist has been the subject of intense critical debate. Yet if the stature of an artist can be measured most truly by his peers' opinion of him, then Griffith's reputation is secure. Sergei Eisenstein clearly admired him; Charles Chaplin believed that 'the whole industry owes its existence to him', while Alfred Hitchcock thought that the basis of film technique was, in some plainly traceable form, the result of Griffith's labors. Frank Capra simply called him 'the poor man's Shakespeare'. Love him or loathe him, Griffith towers over the cinema's early years like a giant.

Griffith was born in Kentucky in 1875 into a family situation that can best be described as one of genteel poverty. Nicknamed 'Roaring Jake' because of his thunderous voice, his father was famous for deeds of heroism as a lieutenant colonel during the Civil War, including taking part in a cavalry charge in a buggy because he had an injured leg. Although he died when the boy was young, Griffith's father bequeathed two characteristics which were to have a considerable influence on his son's artistic development. The first, unsurprisingly, was a fierce pride in the history and values of the American South, which was to surface controversially in Griffith's first masterpiece, THE BIRTH OF A NATION, and for which a number of commentators have never forgiven him. The second was his love of Victorian literature, which not only influenced Griffith's choice of work for adaptation (unusually among his fellow American directors, Griffith chose from such authors as Dickens, Tennyson and Browning), but also influenced the florid and sentimental prose style of Griffith's intertitles which became one of the

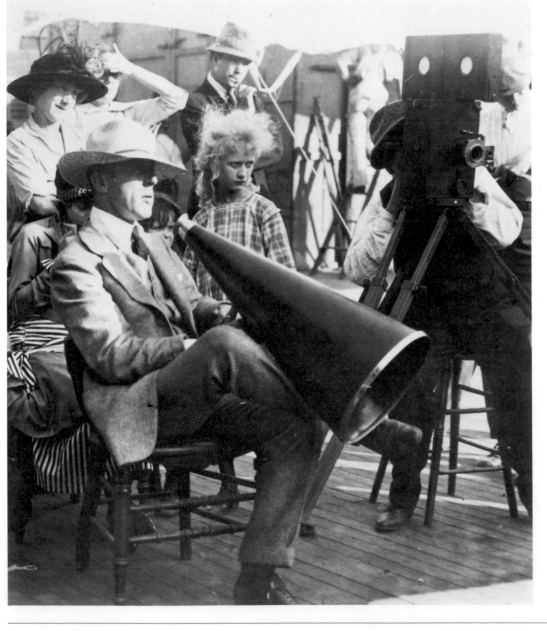

LEFT: D W Griffith, with his megaphone, directing *Intolerance*.

RIGHT: Described by director Allan Dwan as the 'leader of the whole business', Griffith was awarded a special Oscar in 1935.

most distinctive features of his films.

Curiously, Griffith showed little interest in the cinema until he was over 30 years old. As a young man, he fancied himself as a poet or dramatist, and for some time struggled precariously and generally unavailingly to make a living as a writer. His only limited success was a play entitled *A Fool and a Girl*, based on his own experience as a hop-picker, which ran for two weeks in 1907 in Washington and Baltimore. It inspired one notice which according to his wife, haunted Griffith: '. . .if one wants to tell the old and beautiful story of redemption of either man or woman through love, it is not necessary to portray the gutter from which they are redeemed'. Struggling to make a living as an actor and playwright and guided by the recommendation of a friend, Griffith applied to the Biograph Film Studio for work to tide him over the periods of unemployment. He had heard they paid $5 a day for acting, and up to $15 for story suggestions. He appeared in a leading role in

Edwin S Porter's RESCUED FROM AN EAGLE'S NEST under his stage name of Lawrence Griffith. Like most actors, he tended to look down on movies as rather a low form and besides, he told his wife, he would not use his real name until he had become famous. The first stage on this road to fame occurred when, after making several story suggestions to Biograph, some of which he sold, he was offered the chance of directing a one reeler, THE ADVENTURES OF DOLLIE (1908). It was the first of around 450 films he was to make at Biograph over the next five years, during which time he perfected his craft and, in so doing, simultaneously helped shape the future and destiny of the cinema.

It is difficult to convey concisely the range of work that Griffith accomplished during this period. He did comedy, westerns, melodrama, and even biopics like EDGAR ALLAN POE, made in 1909 as a tribute to a writer whom Griffith called 'the most original poetic genius America ever produced'. Five years

later he was also to do a version of Poe's *The Tell Tale Heart* entitled THE AVENGING CONSCIENCE. This film gave some impression of how Griffith's own poetic genius was evolving, as he began to use close ups of feet, hands, objects in a sophisticated tapestry of expressive effect to convey a character's inner state of mind. Other literary giants who received the Griffith treatment included Tolstoy (a 1909 version of the novel, RESURRECTION compressed into a single reel); Tennyson (ENOCH ARDEN, 1909); Dickens (THE CRICKET ON THE HEARTH, 1913); and Browning (PIPPA PASSES in 1911). Significantly, he also began to gather around him his own repertory company of technicians and actors, the most important of whom included the cameraman Billy Bitzer and actresses Dorothy and Lillian Gish, and Mae Marsh. Among other famous personalities who at this stage passed through Griffith's company were Mary Pickford, Douglas Fairbanks, Mack Sennett, Erich von Stroheim and Raoul Walsh.

Griffith might have been expanding his material and augmenting his team, but pre-eminently he was finding a style and developing film technique. More than anyone at this time, Griffith began to free the screen from the conventions of stage melodrama. Previously the convention was simply to stage a scene in front of a static camera, as if the camera were simply a spectator in the theater: one scene equaled one shot. The theatricality of the device inevitably had the effect of inducing a theatricality in performance also. But Griffith, perhaps sensitive to criticisms made of his own acting that it was overly melodramatic, encouraged his actors to tone down their performances for the more intimate requirements of the camera. Moreover, he began to introduce novel elements into his staging of scenes. He included inserts (at this stage he preferred that term to 'close-up'). He experimented with cutting back and forth between different events, crosscutting between rich and poor in A CORNER OF WHEAT (1909), for example. If Dickens could do it in his novels, thought Griffith, why could he not do it in his films? With his cameraman Bitzer, he began to develop atmospheric lighting for mood; and in a film called AFTER MANY YEARS (1908), he incorporated what was then a startling jump in continuity, cutting from a wife as she thinks of her husband to the husband himself, many miles away on a desert island. It was feared that such a leap would leave audiences confused, but they seemed to take Griffith's concept in their stride.

With devices such as this, Griffith was aiming for more than just an increasingly sophisticated way of telling a story. According to his assistant Karl Brown, Griffith's highest objective at this time was 'to photograph thought'. As an example Brown quoted the

moment in JUDITH OF BETHULIA (1914) in which the eponymous heroine momentarily hesitates as she is preparing to murder Holofernes in cold blood. The screen is then filled with the mangled bodies of her own people whom her prospective victim has murdered; her face fills with hate; the deed is done. Nowadays the technique might seem elementary, but at the time it was as if the camera was reading a character's mind as well as recording a character's actions: the impact was considerable. Gradually the hallmarks of a Griffith film began to be discernible. Themes, motifs and characteristics began to recur: the idealization of love, the sentimentalization of the child, the obsession with Civil War subjects that glorified the South, the self-conscious literary pretentions that revealed themselves either in the titles or in the choice of subject matter. Stating that 'I borrowed the cut-back from Charles Dickens', he began to make a speciality of last-minute rescue scenes, in such films as THE LONELY VILLA (1909) and the THE LONEDALE OPERATOR (1911). He might have picked this up from his mentor Edwin S Porter, and he certainly bequeathed this as an idea that had comic potential to one of the writers on these films, Mack Sennett. The device is at the heart of some of Grif-

fith's own most famous set-pieces, notably the thunderously exciting finales of INTOLERANCE (1916) and WAY DOWN EAST (1920). He also began filming on location. THE MUSKETEERS OF PIG ALLEY (1912) was a striking example, perhaps the first gangster movie; filmed in real New York settings, it provided a Dickensian view of the modern city as a vast, impersonal, nightmarish labyrinth.

In 1910, like many other film-makers, Griffith had moved to California, partly to avoid the prohibitive actions against independents of the New York-based Motion Pictures Patent Company and partly because of the more favorable climate for filming. Another important step was Griffith's expansion into the area of the two-reel film, notably in a spectacular western about Custer's Last Stand, THE MASSACRE (1912). It is distinguished by dynamic editing, superb panoramic vistas and a way of distributing cavalrymen in the frame that seemed to presage John Ford. To Griffith's chagrin, the film passed by virtually unnoticed, upstaged by the productions of Adolph Zukor's Famous Players Company which, as its name suggested, filmed some of the leading stage actors of the day in some of their famous theatrical performances. He was also upstaged by the interest in Italian epics such as QUO VADIS? (1912), whose success seemed to indicate a readiness among the public for longer films. When Griffith on his own initiative made the four-reel JUDITH OF BETHULIA (1914), and a piqued Biograph refused for a year to

ABOVE: Henry B Walthall and Blanche Sweet in *Judith of Bethulia*, Griffith's first attempt at an epic that brought him into conflict with the heads at Biograph.

RIGHT: Lillian Gish (left) in *The Musketeers of Pig Alley*, filmed on location in the New York slums.

release it on the grounds of its length, the stage was set for the parting of the ways between Griffith and Biograph. It was the end of an era.

Two things particularly should be stressed about the Griffith divorce from Biograph. The first is the reason for his departure. The disagreement over JUDITH OF BETHULIA – his insistence that it should be a four-reel and not a two-reel film – signaled his determination not to be cowed or confined by convention. After three decades of frustration as an actor and writer, Griffith knew he had found his rightful metier as a film director and probably felt he had no time to waste. This infant art form seemed to unleash the ambition and adventurousness within him that had previously lain dormant, and he was now moving toward an expansion of film form, not only in terms of length but in terms of maturity of theme and grandeur of expression. One might think of him at this time as the Gustav Mahler of the cinema. Mahler said: 'A symphony is like the world, it must embrace everything.' Griffith was rapidly moving towards a similar credo for the film. It meant not only embracing the whole gamut of expressive cinematic devices – close-up, deep-focus, creative montage, split-screen, dissolves, long-shot, camera movement, feature-length narrative – but the selection of subject-matter worthy of such extended treatment. More than anyone working in the

cinema at that time, Griffith felt that film was developing into a new universal language. If that were so, he believed its goal should be nothing less than the brotherhood of man.

The second significant thing about Griffith leaving Biograph was the manner of his departure. It was heralded by a full-page advertisement in the *New York Dramatic Mirror* (3 December 1913), which proceeded to list some of his greatest achievements and described him as 'the producer of all great Biograph successes, revolutionizing Motion Picture drama and founding the modern technique of the art'. False modesty was never one of Griffith's failings, but there is no doubt that this kind of contrived, adulatory publicity contributed to the critical backlash against Griffith, when he began to falter during the 1920s. Was he really the man who invented the language of the cinema or, as more recent film historians have suggested, did he simply have the most industrious and imaginative press agent? The important question remains not when or whether Griffith 'introduced' or 'invented' this or that expressive

The Birth of a Nation.
BELOW: An unnervingly realistic battle scene.

RIGHT: Griffith claimed that

extras totaled 35,000; less extravagant estimates were only 500. This enhances Griffith's achievement, of course.

device, but how well he used it. In this respect, the critical debate over Griffith must concentrate on his two most famous spectacular – and controversial – achievements, THE BIRTH OF A NATION (1915) and IN-TOLERANCE (1916).

If THE BIRTH OF A NATION is commonly regarded as the first masterpiece of the cinema screen, it should also be said that it is also widely regarded as one of the cinema's most unpalatable works. Based on Thomas Dixon's novel, *The Clansman*, whose rampant racism makes it virtually unreadable today (Leslie Fiedler has described it as the worst American novel ever written), THE BIRTH OF A NATION was a drama of the Civil War and its aftermath. President

Woodrow Wilson called it 'history written in lightning'. The Civil War, the assassination of President Lincoln, the continuing bitterness in the aftermath of the war between North and South was seen as if in a fevered dream (remember Griffith carried the whole film round in his head, without recourse to a written script). The spectacle, such as Sherman's march to the sea, was awesome; the pathos of the soldier's homecoming to his devastated home and his reunion with his mother were heart-rending; and the authenticity of the battle scenes, done in the style of Matthew Brady photographs, was frightening. James Agee was to call the opening of the battle scene 'the most beautiful single shot I have ever seen

in any movie'. Equally memorable were the quiet moments, such as the shot of the dead soldier on the battlefield, curled up like a child in sleep, with the simple, ironic title: 'War's Peace'. The superb cast included Donald Crisp, Lillian Gish, Mae Marsh, Wallace Reid, Elmo Lincoln (who was later to be the screen's first Tarzan) and two especially significant roles for two budding directors: Raoul Walsh as John Wilkes Booth in Griffith's celebrated reconstruction of the murder of President Lincoln at the theater, and John Ford as a bespectacled member of the Ku Klux Klan, riding to rescue the honor and maidenhood of the American South.

It was the portrayal of the Klan and negroes which instantly embroiled the film in controversy. No matter that the film's racism was considerably toned down from the novel, and that the film balanced hateful negroes with sympathetic ones, and good whites with bad whites, the film's view of the nation's birth was irredeemably impregnated with the attitudes of a man still wedded to the values and allegiances of the old South. For all its brilliant technique – indeed, many would come to say because of its brilliant technique – the film was denounced in some states as dangerous racism, and it was banned in Chicago, St Louis and Atlantic City. The notoriety only assisted the film's earning power, and it was a

huge box office success: in more ways than one, it was the GONE WITH THE WIND of its day. The film was a milestone, certainly, but one which, to paraphrase the views of black novelist James Baldwin, had the mentality of a lynch mob.

Stung by the attempted suppression of his film, Griffith responded by writing a pamphlet entitled 'The Rise and Fall of Free Speech in America'. But even then, it is probable that he felt he could best answer his critics not with a pen but with a camera. This slowly germinated into the concept behind his next epic film, INTOLERANCE (1916), which as its opening titles tell us, considers 'how hatred and intolerance, through all the ages, have battled against love and charity'. The innovation behind the structure was Griffith's decision to intertwine four stories from different periods of history, bound together by a common theme; and also by what Griffith described as the image of 'a fairy girl with sunlit hair – her hand on the cradle endlessly rocking.' It was an image of humanity inspired by the lines from Walt Whitman's poem, *Leaves of Grass*: '. . . Endlessly rocks the cradle/Uniter of here and hereafter'.

The four stories were: a modern tale of heartless employers and moral reformers, in which a young labor leader is sentenced to death after a strike riot; the massacre of the Huguenots in 1572 on St Bartholomew's Day; the fall of Babylon to the Persians; and the Crucifixion of Christ. All the stories would exemplify aspects of human and social intolerance (though, possibly deliberately, Griffith left racial intolerance out of the picture) and structurally would interact with, and enlarge the significance and resonance of, each other. 'The stories will begin like four currents looked at from a hilltop', said Griffith. 'At first the currents will flow apart, slowly and quietly. But as they flow, they grow nearer and nearer together, and faster and faster, until in the end, in the last act, they mingle in one mighty river of expressed emotion'. The film was made on a huge scale lasting over three hours, but the concept was once again carried in Griffith's head without a shooting script. The titles were written by Anita Loos, who was later to write *Gentlemen Prefer Blondes* and who recalled that her favorite for Griffith's film was a quote she filched from Voltaire: when women cease to attract men, they take to noble deeds to gain attention. The fervor and realism of the strike sequences in the modern story were to have an enormous impact on the young Soviet director, Sergei Eisenstein, whilst his compatriot Pudovkin was equally impressed by Griffith's attention to performance and detail, notably the famous shot of Mae Marsh's clenched hands to suggest her tension during the murder trial of her husband.

LEFT: Lillian Gish (second from right) appearing in *The Birth of a Nation*.

TOP RIGHT: The hero (Robert Harron) about to be saved from execution in the modern story of *Intolerance*.

RIGHT: The Christ story in *Intolerance*, with Howard Gaye as the Christ.

Inevitably though, most attention was given to the spectacle of the Babylon story, particularly the set of the Babylonian palace, designed by Walter L Hall, with its 165-foot-high towers, ramparts strong enough to withstand the weight of thundering chariots and with 4000 extras required for the set piece of Belshazzar's Feast. The film was a technical tour-de-force, with varied editing rhythms, an alternation between close detail and epic detachment, adroit use of masking the sides of the film frame to vary the size of the image for dramatic effect, and a powerful presentation of violence (notably a moment when an opponent is decapitated during the Fall of Babylon sequence) that still has the power to shock. It was to traditional film narrative what Beethoven's 'Eroica' had been to the classical symphony: an expressive breakthrough that, in its grandeur of conception and theme, annihilated all previous formal boundaries.

Yet, although subsequent generations of film historians have judged it to be a finer work than THE BIRTH OF A NATION, INTOLERANCE was not a success. Contemporary audiences seemed to have been a bit bewildered by the style, feeling that the inter-mingled four stories, far from expanding each other's significance, got in each other's way. What it lacked in comparison with BIRTH OF A NATION was emotional involvement. The spectacle of Babylonian battle was stirring enough, but it would have been more exciting if you could have cared who won. It was also felt that, like a latter-day epic HEAVEN'S GATE (1980), whose critical attitude to the Western came at a time when America was searching for a recuperation of national myths, INTOLERANCE was a victim of bad timing. It was peddling the wrong message at the wrong time, its implicit pacifism striking a jarring note at a time when America was readying itself for war.

A modern film historian, David Shipman has bluntly opined that the film 'has virtually no entertainment value'. The mass film audience of the time might have shared that view, though as an aesthetic criterion it has its limitations. 'Entertainment value'

BELOW: The immense Babylon set for *Intolerance*. which must have accounted for a large part of the films $2.5 million cost.

RIGHT: The fall of Babylon as directed by Griffith.

is not in abundant supply in a work like Milton's *Paradise Lost* but it is still a great epic – and so is INTOLERANCE. François Truffaut once made the interesting observation that 'all great films are failures', because they are invariably ahead of, rather than in tune with, their times and their qualities only therefore become gradually apparent. Also they refuse to conform to the conventions of 'public art', which is the reason that contemporary audiences and critics have difficulty in coming to terms with them. For Erich von Stroheim, INTOLERANCE was the film in which Griffith 'had put beauty and poetry into a cheap and tawdry sort of amusement'. Its influence on the next generation of film-makers was to be profound; Stroheim and King Vidor drew on its social realism and its observations on human psychology, Eisenstein and Pudovkin studied and learnt from its miracles of montage, and De Mille and Abel Gance were inspired by its sensuality and creative megalomania.

Griffith made one other great film during this decade, BROKEN BLOSSOMS (1919). For those who find the epic Griffith a little hard to take, this might even be his greatest achievement, for it is as concentrated and compelling as the other two are grandiose and rambling. 'It is as if Dickens had spoken by means of the camera', said a contemporary reviewer of the film: certain outlines of the plot do bear a similarity to Dickens's *Little Dorritt*. The movie told the story of the love that blossoms between a Chinaman (Richard Barthelmess) and a young girl (Lillian Gish) who is being ill treated by her father (Donald Crisp). Like Dickens, Griffith was unafraid of melodrama and stirred by the plight of the downtrodden. This 'tale of tears', set in a fog-cloaked London, developed into a titanic, three-way struggle between compassion, innocence and brutality. As the 'child with a tear-aged face', whose growth seems stunted by her domestic prison, Lillian Gish gave what is assuredly one of the most memorable performances of the silent era. Her hysteria in the closet as she tries to hide from her murderous father was a cameo of naked fear that terrified contemporary audiences. Yet Griffith's other

LEFT: The St Bartholomew's Day massacre in *Intolerance*, Griffith's example of the extremes of religious intolerance.

RIGHT: Griffith's favorite actress, Lillian Gish in perhaps her greatest role, *Broken Blossoms*.

BELOW: China sequence from *Broken Blossoms*.

films during this period seemed to suggest that his grip was beginning to slip. Two films about the war – HEARTS OF THE WORLD (1918) and ISN'T LIFE WONDER-FUL? (1924) – will be discussed in greater detail in a subsequent chapter, but neither was especially popular with audiences. Griffith's greatest hit at this time was WAY DOWN EAST (1920), chiefly memorable for the exciting last reel in which Lillian Gish is rescued on the ice; and in ORPHANS OF THE STORM (1922), the Gish sisters were pitched with some success into the French Revolution.

Griffith's business deals were going awry. After the losses incurred on INTOLERANCE, Griffith had to part company in 1917 with the Triangle Corporation which he had joined with Thomas Ince and Mack Sennett. Five years after forming United Artists in 1919 with Charles Chaplin, Douglas Fairbanks and Mary Pickford, amid much publicity and quips to the effect that 'the lunatics had taken over the asylum', Griffith left the company in some acrimony to work for Paramount. It was a bad move that produced no major work. The irony was that, although Griffith's earlier work was now having a considerable influence on 1920s' film-making, notably in the drive toward greater realism and the recognition of the creative potential of film editing, his own productions of this period suddenly looked very old-fashioned. Somehow the sense of him as an anachronism was heightened by his confident pronouncement in 1924 that: 'We do not want now and we never shall want the human voice with our films. . . Music – fine music – will always be the voice of the silent drama'. It is hardly surprising then that, when sound came to the cinema, Griffith was somewhat taken aback, and his own sound films, ABRAHAM LINCOLN (1930), starring Walter Huston, and a drama of alcohol addiction, THE STRUGGLE (1931), were dismissed as stilted and theatrical. In fact, the latter film in particular warrants rediscovery: in places it has poignancy and a raw authenticity. Griffith's final years before his death in 1948, were spent in relative obscurity. In one of his last interviews, he expressed an admiration for contemporary directors like Preston Sturges and John Ford, and a love for Orson Welles's CITIZEN KANE 'for the ideas he took from me', but, for the most part, he gave the impression of a saddened man, an erstwhile innovator over-taken by events. The cinema had eventually passed him by.

Since his death, there has been the inevitable reaction against his reputation. For all the technical innovation, some have said Griffith was essentially an old-fashioned personality and his films are rooted in the attitudes of the nineteenth rather than the twentieth century, which is the reason that they have not been successfully revived. Conversely, others have

TOP LEFT: Donald Crisp as the brutal father in *Broken Blossoms*.

BOTTOM LEFT: Lillian Gish about to fall through the ice in *Way Down East*, which set off one of Griffith's most exciting rescue scenes.

RIGHT: Walter Huston (seated at foreground) in the title role of *Abraham Lincoln*, Griffith's first film of the sound era.

praised his unusual sensitivity, his incorporation of thoughtful themes into mainstream cinema, and his improvement of the standards of screen performance, simply through his concentration on the face of the actor more than the gesture. In all these ways he stimulated an audience's imagination. The writer and critic Susan Sontag has compared Griffith with the eighteenth century English novelist Samuel Richardson (author of *Pamela* and *Clarissa*): both moralistic men who discovered psychology in their respective art forms, they were acutely sensitive to feminine feeling and were morbidly preoccupied with the situation of virginal innocence in danger of violation by brute seducers. One senses something of Griffith's 'feminine' sensitivity in another artist of the American South who sometimes shared his themes, Tennessee Williams. A STREETCAR NAMED DESIRE has a very Griffith-like feeling to it, particularly the Griffith of BROKEN BLOSSOMS: an air of mor-

bidity and melodrama, but also an enormous compassion for the vulnerable, the sensitive, and the delicate.

D W Griffith was a pathfinder. He sought greater realism in cinema, with a resultant enrichment of performance and complexity of characterization; and he sought the truth. He might not have been the first to deploy editing creatively in film, but no one understood more thoroughly than Griffith how editing could be exploited for expressive ends nor saw quite so clearly how important it was to film aesthetics. Nobody had more influence than Griffith on the future of the narrative film, and it was Griffith more than anyone else, who suggested the extraordinary propagandist potential of film. Above all, Griffith was the man who gave the cinema artistic respectability. For a limited but golden period, he was the cinema's first director superstar; its first *auteur*; its first emperor.

ABOVE: Mack Sennet

CHAPTER THREE

King of
Keystone

'To the master of fun, discoverer of stars, the
sympathetic, kindly, understanding comedy genius,
Mack Sennett, for his lasting contribution to the
comedy technique of the screen'. (Special Oscar
awarded to Sennett in 1937.)

Sennett, whose real name was Michael Sinnott, was born in 1880 in Quebec to working class Irish immigrants. As a young man he had a variety of jobs, including that of boilermaker, before going into showbusiness. His earliest theatrical specialty was the portrayal of a comic policeman, which was undoubtedly the genesis of the Keystone Kops. Whereas in Chaplin and Keaton the police were often figures of fear as well as fun, in Sennett they were subjected to affectionate ridicule as well-meaning authority figures who, unfortunately, just cannot be trusted to do an efficient job.

On joining Biograph, Sennett worked as an actor for D W Griffith, whom he came to revere. 'He was my day school, my adult education program, my professor', Sennett said of Griffith in his ghosted autobiography, *King of Comedy*. It is interesting to think of Sennett's films in relation to Griffith's, where the seriousness of theme and purposes of the latter's work are duplicated by Sennett but in farcical form. Like Griffith's films, Sennett's were often rooted in reality, but he pushed this to comic rather than tragic lengths. From Griffith, Sennett learnt the art of editing, of cutting pictures sharply to inject pace into them, except that whereas Griffith's chases were full of suspense, Sennett's were hilarious. The point is graphically apparent in the difference between a film Sennett wrote for Griffith, THE LONELY VILLA, which has a thrilling rescued-in-time finale, and a film Sennett was later to make himself in 1912, HELP! HELP!, where the same situation is pushed to the point of parody.

The story of Sennett's move into production is rather a complicated one. One reason was simply that he was not a very good actor, and he also clearly wanted more control over his scripts. Sennett had a

LEFT: Mack Sennett in a small role in one of his own comedy shorts in 1913, outside a cinema advertising a Keystone comedy.

RIGHT: Sennett's favorite leading lady: Mabel Normand.

Sincerely Mabel Normand

colorful story to tell about the way in which he acquired Keystone Studios: essentially by sweet-talking a couple of ex-bookies, Adam Kessel and Charles Baumann, into writing off his gambling debts and investing in this film venture. The story, unfortunately, is not quite true. Kessel and Baumann were actually quite experienced independent film producers at this time, responsible for a number of Thomas Ince productions for their Bison Film Company. Rather than being alternately bemused and bedazzled by Sennett's Irish charm, they probably saw his proposal as a good investment. Very quickly Sennett imported a whole bevy of talented players from Biograph to work under his Keystone roof, including Ford Sterling, Mabel Normand, Roscoe

'Fatty' Arbuckle, Chester Conklin and Ben Turpin. Soon the team was joined by a young star from English music hall making a start in movies – Charles Chaplin.

In the following years, Sennett was also to further the careers of such prodigious talents as Gloria Swanson and Carole Lombard and, in the sound era (by which time Sennett had moved to Paramount), Bing Crosby and W C Fields. Small wonder that the Oscar citation referred to him as the 'discoverer of stars'. Only Buster Keaton of the major silent comedians does not seem to have come under Sennett's aegis at some time or another. One of the few whose talent he failed to recognize was Harold Lloyd, whom he sacked because he did not think he was

ABOVE: Mabel Normand and Fatty Arbuckle. The careers of both were to be blighted by scandal.

TOP AND BOTTOM RIGHT: The chaotic Keystone Kops bite the dust.

funny. It was Hal Roach, whom Sennett described as 'my only rival', who was to tap the comic potential of Lloyd.

Although Sennett was unrivaled as a 'discoverer' of talent, it is noticeable that many were to leave him to work on their own. In the case of someone like Chaplin, this was an understandable development, since his particular genius would clearly crave greater creative freedom and independence. In some cases though, the departures had much to do with Sennett's own personality. He was not only volatile and stingy – he could also be domineering and autocratic. He created a somewhat fearsome persona for himself, with many strange and intimidating idiosyncrasies. He had a bath in his office which reputedly, he would sit in at some stage every day, pondering ideas and trying to generate inspiration. He also had a rocking chair in the projection room where he sat to watch the rough assemblages of his movies. Employees learnt to interpret the movements of the rocking chair with some trepidation. If it did not rock during Sennett's viewing of a film comedy, then the movie and the director were in trouble.

The essence of Sennett's comedy was movement. In this, it was a comedy that seemed fundamentally filmic. For a number of artists and critics of the time,

Sennett's cinema was preferable to Griffith's. Whereas Griffith's work, they said, reeked of noble intentions and the melodrama of the Victorian stage, Sennett's work was blessedly vulgar, flying in the face of good taste, and seemed more attuned to the manic energy of the modern age. Yet, as well as being more truly a product of the age, Sennett's films also sent it up. The machine age was made to look comically absurd. This was particularly so in a Keystone chase where – and here Sennett always acknowledged the influential pioneering work of early French comedians and film-makers, such as Zecca and Linder – cars, trains, coaches would hurtle with hair-raising hilarity in increasingly improbable directions. Sennett's films, unlike Griffith's, were invariably set in the America of the early twentieth century but this recognizable world was quickly revealed to be slightly mad, and the comedy thus had an intriguing combination of being down-to-earth and at the same time close to wild fantasy. The critics

ABOVE: The brush moustache was his trademark: Billy Bevan, who appeared in 70 Sennett shorts in the 1920s.

LEFT: Gloria Swanson in *Teddy at the Throttle*, one of her early roles for Sennett.

RIGHT: Salacious reading matter for Fatty Arbuckle.

Richard Griffith and Arthur Mayer described Sennett's world well when they defined its principal feature as being the fact that 'nothing in it had normal consequences. . . people could do things that in real life would have the most catastrophic effects. They are the things we all wish to do without daring to do – hence the primary appeal of Sennett's work'.

The vintage period of Keystone Koppery was relatively short-lived, and they never advanced much beyond the frenzy of an early work, IN THE CLUTCHES OF A GANG (1913), which remained an unsurpassed demonstration of the Keystone style. LOVE, SPEED AND THRILLS (1915) was the title of one of the Keystone films and that was what they offered – generally in reverse order. In SNOOKIE'S FLIRTATION (1912), Sennett's top star of the time, Ford Sterling, whose half-beard on his chin always gave him the appearance of a pantomime villain, causes chaos when he gets a job in a shoe shop. Gloria Swanson had her first starring role in Sennett's THE PULLMAN BRIDE (1916); and his star comedienne, Mabel Normand, to whom Sennett was devoted, did a spirited imitation of Pearl White in her PERILS OF PAULINE adventures when, in BARNEY OLDFIELD'S RACE FOR LIFE (1914), Mabel finds herself tied to the railway tracks by villains as a train moves ever closer.

In an interview in 1915, Sennett described his method of work as follows: 'Having found your hub idea, you build out the spokes; those are the natural developments that your imagination will suggest. Then introduce your complications that make up the funny wheel. . .' The mechanical imagery is very revealing here, for he did seem to see his movies as a kind of mechanism in which the engine was the basic idea, on which all kinds of embellishments of detail, gesture and action could be hung. 'We have tried famous humorists', Sennett remarked, 'and I can say with feeling that their stuff is about the worst we get'. What he preferred was an engine room of gag-men, each trying to top the other. A young member of the 'Gag Room', as it was called, was Frank Capra who, in the next decade, was to make some of Harry Langdon's biggest successes, and subsequently to make some of the classic films of the American screen, such as MR SMITH GOES TO WASHINGTON (1938) and IT'S A WONDERFUL LIFE (1946). In his autobiography, THE NAME ABOVE THE TITLE Capra gave one illuminating example of the way the Gag Room worked. As a joke, one of the writers had rung up Sennett to say cross-eyed comic Ben Turpin had gone to a doctor to get his eyes straightened. Sennett had threatened to shoot every doctor in Hollywood. 'Say', said one gag man, 'let's use that as a basis of a story: Turpin seeing a doctor to get his eyes straightened. . .' 'Then', said another, 'all the doctors in town end up cross eyed. . .' Idea, plus

snowballing complications, taken to the extreme of absurdity: Sennett's structural principle in a nut shell.

In addition to speed and the chase, Sennett had one other vital ingredient for madcap comedy: the custard pie. It was never actually custard, which was too pale to photograph: it was more often a sickly concoction of blackberries or paste, topped with whipped cream. According to Sennett, the real inventor of the custard pie at the Keystone Studio was Mabel Normand who, to liven up a scene in A NOISE FROM THE DEEP (1913) in which Fatty Arbuckle had his head stuck through a door, picked up the remaining contents of a workman's lunch and lobbed it nonchalantly in the actor's face. 'It was funny,' said Sennett, 'not only because a pie in the face is an outrage to pumped up dignity, but because the actor received the custard without a flicker of premonition.' That description is significant because, perhaps unconsciously, Sennett pinpointed the two essential ingredients of his comedy: aggression and surprise.

Soon, the story went, a man called Greenburg had become rich through making inedible paste-filled Throwing Pies for Sennett movies. The champion pie-thrower on the lot was reckoned to be the ambidextrous Fatty Arbuckle, who could hit a target with either right or left hand at a distance of ten yards. After the death in 1915 of the Pickwickian John

LEFT: Roscoe 'Fatty' Arbuckle, one of the most inventive of silent comedians.

ABOVE: Marie Dressler (left), watched by Charles Chaplin and Mabel Normand, in a manic moment from *Tillie's Punctured Romance*.

Bunny, who worked for Vitagraph Studios in films such as VANITY FAIR (1911), PICKWICK PAPERS (1913) and BUNNY IN BUNNYLAND (1915), Arbuckle was to become the screen's most popular 'fat man' comedian, with a physical agility that belied his bulk (rather in the way that Oliver Hardy's burly frame was to be comically offset by the delicacy of his hand movements and the subtlety of his facial expressions). Arbuckle went into direction, nurturing the talent of a young Buster Keaton, before becoming embroiled in a sex scandal that was to shake Hollywood to its foundations.

With the phenomenal rival popularity of Chaplin and the later emergence in the 1920s of such extraordinarily gifted film comedians as Keaton, Langdon and Lloyd, Sennett's crown as the king of comedy began to slip. His involvement with the Triangle Film Corporation alongside Griffith and Thomas Ince had not been a success, and it was clear that his frenetic style would have to be modified in order to make itself adaptable to the developing taste for longer films. Two reels of frenzy were fine, but ten would be very tiring. Nevertheless, as early as 1914, Sennett had made a feature length film, TILLIE'S PUNCTURED ROMANCE, with Chaplin, Mabel Normand and Marie Dressler, which had been a great success. Sennett was nothing if not adaptable. If his crazy slapstick was now either too crazy for the time or being better done elsewhere, maybe he could smuggle something of the old eccentricity into the titles. 'The restaurant was so small', said one memorable title, 'they had to serve condensed milk. . .'

In addition to his Bathing Beauties who somehow seemed emblematic of the flapper era and of a decade that really roared, Sennett's biggest star of the 1920s was Ben Turpin. Sennett thought Turpin had something of the universal appeal of a Chaplin or a Langdon: what he called 'the appeal of all undersized gents who stand up against Fate any-

In 1928 Sennett made LOVE AT FIRST FLIGHT which poked fun at Charles Lindbergh and his historic flight to Paris, but the joke was rather upstaged by a cartoon on the same theme, PLANE CRAZY (1928) which featured one of the first screen appearances of a mouse called Mickey. With the coming of sound, it was Disney who began to dominate the market of the one-reel and two-reel comedy; and the anarchic visual attack of the old Sennett gave way to the iconoclastic verbal volleys of the Marx Brothers, at their best in a film like DUCK SOUP (1932), directed by one of Hal Roach's protegés from the silent era, Leo McCarey. By the mid 1930s, Sennett had gracefully eased his way out of film production and, apart from the odd personal appearance in films such as HOLLYWOOD CAVALCADE (1939) and DOWN MEMORY LANE (1949), he retired from the screen. He died in 1960.

Sennett's contribution to screen comedy was to prompt a number of memorials in a different vein. One was a series of feature-length film anthologies including DAYS OF THRILLS AND LAUGHTER (1960) and WHEN COMEDY WAS KING (1960), compiled by Robert Youngson, which paid tribute to the impolite but good-natured antics of Sennett style comedy. These

way'. This was overstating the case. The humor of Turpin was less dependent on character than on context. He was hilarious as a spoof Rudolph Valentino in THE SHRIEK OF ARABY (1923) and in WHEN A MAN'S A PRINCE (1926), he was equally and superbly incongruous as a mock Prussian officer, like Erich von Stroheim with (very) roving eyes. At this time Sennett's main comic component was not the chase, but the parody of popular successes. For example, THE HOLLYWOOD KID (1924), about a rival film company trying to entice a child star, was undoubtedly partly inspired by the enormous success of Chaplin's THE KID (1921) and his young child star, Jackie Coogan. It was a beguiling production nevertheless, featuring such regulars as Turpin, Ford Sterling and even the famous Keystone lion, and offering the novelty of a tour of the Keystone Studio. One senses that, by this time, Sennett was living off old memories more than attempting anything really fresh.

RIGHT: Phyllis Haver with Jimmy Finlayson, two of Sennett's most popular performers.

LEFT: Phyllis Haver, one of Hollywood's most sought-after glamour queens until her retirement in 1929.

BELOW: The Sennett bathing beauties, with Santa.

brought the Keystone Kops hurtling into the path of a new generation of cinema-goers, and showed that Sennett was the master of delivering peril with panache. Another tribute came in the form of a musical *Mack and Mabel* written by *Hello Dolly!* composer Jerry Herman, produced on Broadway in 1974 and with Robert Preston playing Sennett. Another homage of a kind to the whole Sennett era was Stanley Kramer's IT'S A MAD, MAD, MAD, MAD WORLD (1963), in which slapstick was given the full Cinerama treatment. All Kramer's film lacked was heart. 'They're all crooks so you don't care if all of them fall', said Hal Roach astutely, contrasting this with a Harold Lloyd situation where 'people are anxious that he doesn't fall, therefore when he slips there's a gasp and when he catches himself there's a laugh...'

Roach's reference to Lloyd is a reminder that, although Sennett might have been the self-styled 'King of Comedy' and the founding father of silent screen mirth, not all the great silent comedians were either his 'subjects' or his 'children'. Indeed one of Sennett's mottos was: 'always a borrower or a lender be', and one of the comedians he borrowed from most was the French comedian, Max Linder. His slapstick was more debonair than frenetic but like Sennett he loved to spin infinite variations on a single theme, as in a film like MAX TAKES A BATH (1915), where stage by logical stage, he goes from taking a bath to being hoisted through Parisian streets by a horde of policemen. Linder's ex-

perience in Hollywood was not a happy one, despite a parody of Douglas Fairbanks's THREE MUS-KETEERS entitled THE THREE MUST-GET-THERES (1922), of which Sennett would have been proud; two years after his return from Hollywood in 1925, he was found dead in a Paris hotel in a suicide pact with his wife.

Harold Lloyd, on the other hand, was for Sennett the one that got away. He could see no comic potential in him and a disillusioned Lloyd returned to Harold Roach, who made him moderately successful in the role of 'Lonesome Luke'; he really hit the jackpot when he scaled down his persona to that of Mr Average America, topped off with a pair of oversized spectacles that were to be the screen's most famous glasses until the advent of Woody Allen. In SAFETY LAST (1923), he was the little man in the big city; in THE FRESHMAN (1925), he was the focus of every sort of campus caper; and in GRANDMA'S BOY (1921), he was a nervous country boy who plucked up courage to tackle a bully in order to win the girl he loved. Lloyd's secret, Roach felt, was the way the

LEFT: Cross-eyed comic, Ben Turpin in a 1926 Sennett production, *A Blonde's Revenge*.

BOTTOM LEFT: Bespectacled but athletic Harold Lloyd in *The Freshman*.

BELOW: Hanging on for dear life: one of Lloyd's most daredevil stunts in *Safety Last*.

ostensible 'bookishness' of his persona, signaled by his owlish spectacles, was suddenly belied by a freakish athleticism that seemed to combine the elements of Fairbanks and farce. But is it not surprising that Sennett missed the humor of Lloyd, who was altogether too gentle a soul for the bulldozing Keystone style.

Whereas Sennett's style was a tendency to pile one thing on top of another to achieve the ultimate comic catharsis, Roach's was more studied. Sennett created chaos better than he created character, whereas Roach's comedy was rooted in humanity. It

was Roach who nurtured a comedy duo who, by the end of the 1920s, had mastered an interplay of opposites, and a multiple variety of nuances on the theme of the fallibility of friendship: Laurel and Hardy. The great thing about them, said Roach, was that they could get three laughs where another comedian would be struggling to get one. For example, if one of them slipped in the mud, the humor would flow not only from the situation itself but also from Ollie Hardy's inimitable expression of disgust, and then from Stan Laurel's equally eloquent look of bewilderment. Nevertheless, one of their best comedies of the silent era, THE BATTLE OF THE CENTURY (1929) – about an argument that escalates into one of pie-throwing mayhem – seemed more in the style of Sennett than Roach. The writer Henry Miller

described it as 'the apotheosis of pie-throwing'. Sennett would probably have described it as custard's last stand.

Sennett's description of another great silent comedian, Harry Langdon, was rather less than generous: 'His cunning as a businessman was about that of a backward kindergarten student and he complicated this with marital adventures in which he was about as inept as he was on the screen'. According to Frank Capra, who wrote one of Langdon's three big hits TRAMP, TRAMP, TRAMP (1926) and directed the other two, THE STRONG MAN (1926) and LONG PANTS (1927), Langdon let his sudden popularity go to his head while simultaneously failing to understand the nature of this appeal, with the result that his decision to assume control over his whole career was an un-

LEFT: Stan (Laurel) has toothache: Ollie (Hardy) is unsympathetic. The opening of *Leave 'em Laughing* (1928).

BOTTOM LEFT: Laurel and Hardy as Christmas tree salesmen in one of their classic shorts, *Big Business*.

RIGHT: Harry Langdon, both lustful and homicidal, in *Long Pants*, directed by Frank Capra.

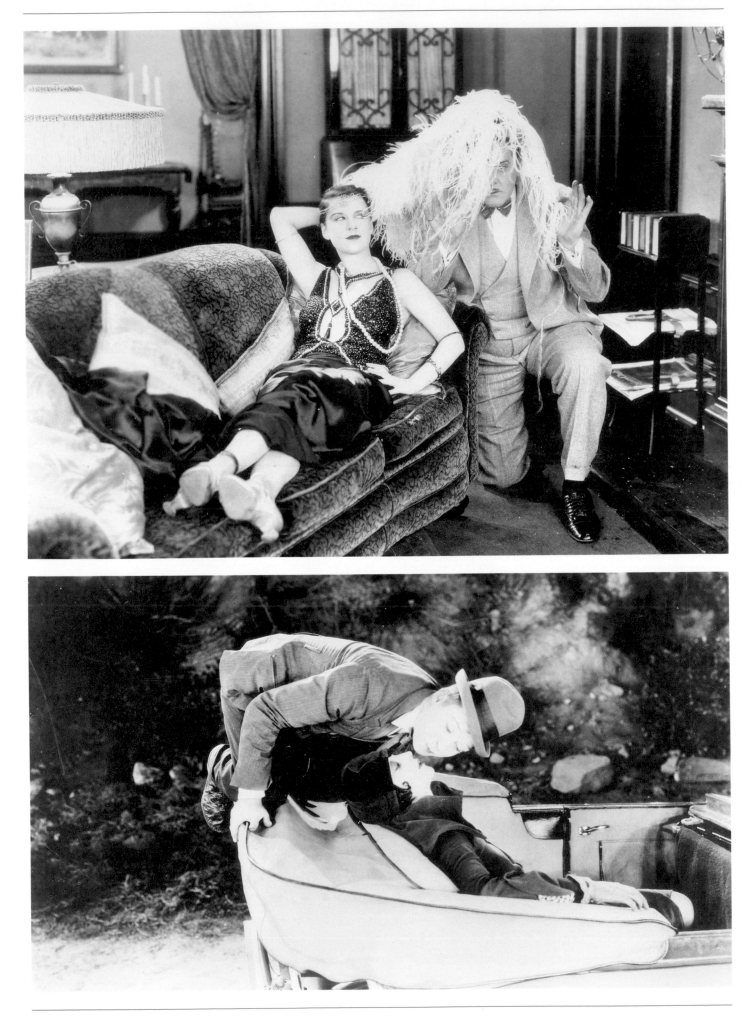

LEFT: Beatrice Lillie and Harry C Myer in the superb backstage comedy, *Exit Smiling*.

RIGHT: Marion Davies, with confectionery missile, in *Show People*.

BOTTOM LEFT: Harry Langdon in his last major hit, *Long Pants*.

BELOW: Langdon plays a simple ex-soldier looking for his pen pal in *The Strong Man*.

mitigated disaster. He thought he had the pathos and range of a Chaplin, when really his persona – a dreamer with a child-like innocence – was more akin to that of Stan Laurel. In fairness, however, it should be added that silent film historian William K Everson condemned Capra's portraiture as 'vindictive'; and an authority on silent screen comedy, Walter Kerr thought Langdon's talent was second only to Keaton.

Of the silent comediennes, none was more vivacious and entrancing than Sennett's own Mabel Normand, though in a style more sophisticated than slapstick, it would be hard to find a more subtly delightful performance than Beatrice Lillie's as an ambitious, love-smitten amateur actress in Samuel Taylor's gentle and affectionate work, EXIT SMILING (1928). Silent comedy was not all frenzy and panic, but when it was, few could surpass the exuberant vulgarity and vitality of Sennett at his peak. He seemed to embody the enthusiasm and energy of an America bursting with a new confidence and with a new gadget it had made uniquely its own: the movie camera.

ABOVE: William S H

CHAPTER FOUR

When Sauerkraut became Liberty Cabbage

'Prior to the war,' Anita Loos explained to
distinguished film historian, Kevin Brownlow,
'European movies were flourishing in Europe,
particularly in France and Italy, and there was no
real need for Hollywood or its product. But when
war broke out, the whole scene changed. It was
impossible to work with the economics of war
surrounding these studios. So I really credit
Hollywood on *World War One*.'

It is true that the outbreak of war in 1914 had a disastrous effect on film production in Europe. Actors were called up, studios requisitioned, investment curtailed, and for a while production came to a standstill. When it did begin again, the films tended to be war-oriented and propagandist in tone, which did not appeal to audiences. It was therefore a great opportunity for American filmmakers to fill this vacuum, and some could hardly resist rubbing their hands with glee at their good fortune.

Nevertheless, it must be emphasized that even without the war, America was poised to become the dominant force in the film industry at this time. It had the advantage of a massive home audience for one thing, one which was mainly working class and with a big immigrant population for whom the movies were not only the cheapest form of entertainment around, but offered no language barrier. Also the film business was tailor-made for the kind of industrial shrewdness and enterprise at which America in this century has always excelled. The trail blazers were businessmen such as Adolph Zukor of Paramount Pictures, William Fox of the Fox Film Company and Marcus Loew of Loews Incorporated (which was later to become MGM). These were some of the men who saw the massive commercial potential of American film and who lost no time in developing film production as a factory system, in which the production, distribution and exhibition of film came under one business organization. For example, by 1921 Paramount owned four hundred cinemas and exhibitors had to take a package of their films, sight unseen, with the promise perhaps of one glittering star vehicle among them. For the studios, the system had the massive advantage of reducing financial risk, and it was a system that survived until the late 1940s.

It should be remembered that American film was not always synonymous with Hollywood. Hollywood did not become the film capital of the world until a good twenty years after the Lumières' first film screening in Paris and, in the early days of cinema, the center of film production in America was New York. At the beginning of the century Hollywood was famous only for its orange and lemon groves. The founding father of Hollywood was a real-estate agent called Harvey Wilcox who

BELOW: A young Cecil B De Mille (right) at work in a suburb of Los Angeles called Hollywood, where he rented half a barn as his studio.

had retired to his fruit ranch on the outskirts of Los Angeles. His wife Deida had met a lady from Chicago whose country home was called Hollywood. Mrs Wilcox liked the name so much that she christened their ranch 'Hollywood' too, and the name stuck even when the ranch was later divided into building lots.

Hollywood's development as the center of the film industry was the direct result of a bitter dispute between independent film producers and a trust called the Motion Picture Patents Company. The latter had been formed in 1909 by the nine major companies in partnership with Thomas Edison and was an endeavor to establish a monopoly over the fast-growing film industry. They patented film apparatus and charged for its use. A cinema owner had to have a license to show films made by any of the nine companies in the Trust and was subject to sanctions if he showed any 'outlaw' product from the independents. The Trust even employed detectives to track down and prosecute any rival who was using equipment patented by them. 'It was ridiculous', said Hollywood veteran Allan Dwan, 'like selling an automobile and not letting anyone else drive it because you have a patent on putting your foot on the pedal'. Yet he remembered rough-necks and gangsters burning down rival facilities in New York, and the Trust even employing snipers with long range rifles to shoot at the cameras (which were expensive and hard to replace). Sometimes an extra would turn out to be a Company spy. Eventually the Trust collapsed because a court in 1916 deemed that its actions amounted to unlawful restraint of trade, but by this time many independents had been forced out of business. Some, however, refused to give in to such harassment and began to move their operations away from New York where the Trust was strongest, to somewhere where its influence was less powerful.

California was an ideal spot. It was near to Mexico, so the independents could make a quick getaway if a Patents Company spy was spotted on the horizon. Also property was much cheaper in California than New York, so economically the move made sense. Above all, it offered perfect conditions for filming. It guaranteed almost unbroken sunshine during the day, and boasted a landscape full of possibilities for picture making: mountains, sky, desert, farmland. In 1914 Cecil B De Mille traveled to Hollywood to make his first feature-length film, THE SQUAW MAN, which turned out to be a huge hit, and further helped to establish Hollywood as the new base for film production.

It is undeniable that the war years, which inevitably reduced competition from Europe, were a business boom to American film producers, but there were other factors which contributed to America's dominance of the film market. It was an industry that in some ways seemed to suit the spirit of the country. It was new, optimistic, polyglot, and had an uncultured vitality unhindered by years of class-bound tradition. It was a period which saw a rapid growth in America of cinema buildings, which again swelled the audiences. In contrast to the old nickelodeons, the first of the modern cinemas for first-run films were often built by film companies for showing their own product and at a higher price for exclusive presentation. One effect of this was obviously to broaden the audience for films, which had previously been predominantly working class, to include a more prosperous, middle class clientele: this in turn would obviously have the effect of influencing content.

One final factor that contributed to the dominance of American films during the war years was the quality of its product. 1914-1918 was one of the golden periods of American film. It included the two massive masterpieces of Griffith, THE BIRTH OF A NATION and INTOLERANCE; the emergence of Thomas Ince and Cecil B De Mille as major directors; Mack Sennett in his prime; the astonishing rise of Charlie Chaplin; and the development of the star power of Mary Pickford. For all the discussion of American film's commercial advantages at this stage, it should not be forgotten that it was also a period that saw an amazing creative outpouring from American directors and performers.

Nevertheless, the war served to crystalize two aspects of the cinema which were extremely important. They might seem obvious points but in the early days of the cinema, they were by no means so apparent. The first was the value of the cinema as a provider of escapism. In time of war, and later during the Depression, people flocked to the cinema to forget their troubles – it was often their main source of relief. The second aspect of film which really emerged during the war years, was its enormous potential for propaganda. This was probably the first time film makers (and also people outside the cinema) realized how powerful a weapon the cinema could be as a means of influencing opinion and arousing emotion. As the critic Robert Sklar has observed in his book *Movie-Made America*, because of the way the sequence was edited, it was hard to resist supporting the Ku Klux Klan in BIRTH OF A NATION as they ride to the rescue of an imperiled white family, even for audiences who might deplore the film's apparent racism and theme of white supremacy. The power of film was such, that in the hands of a master like Griffith, it could overwhelm reason. Films made during and about the Great War were to bear this lesson very much in

mind, and were to become very interesting on one level as barometers of public opinion. The shift in America's attitude to the war, from pacifism and neutrality to militarism and aggressive involvement, can be clearly traced through the films of the period.

In terms of escapism, one of the most popular film forms of the period was the Western. It was a genre that had flourished reasonably well since Porter's THE GREAT TRAIN ROBBERY, but clearly the shift of film production from the urbanized East Coast of New York and New Jersey to the more rugged and unspoiled West Coast of California aided authenticity. It was also probable that in a war period of complexity and confusion, the straightforward morality tales of the Western of good versus evil had a particular appeal. The great Western star of the war years was William S Hart, who began working for Thomas Ince but directed himself in what were probably his two best films, HELL'S HINGES (1916) and THE NARROW TRAIL (1917). He was later to be upstaged by Tom Mix who offered more spectacular action in his Westerns. Hart offered a more 'adult'

Western through his development of a character who had elements of corruption in his personality but who was subsequently redeemed either by love of by some noble deed. His films appealed to both the critics and the public, for they were thoughtful enough to warrant attention but exciting enough to provide traditional escapist entertainment. The period also saw the first feature-length Western of John Ford, STRAIGHT SHOOTING (1917), which combined Griffith's visual sense with a strong human story (within its cattleman versus farmer formula) that had all the virtues of Hart.

The other most popular form of escapist entertainment during the war years was the serial adventure. For companies which were nervous at this time about making the transition from two-reelers to feature-length films, the serial was a splendid compromise; and with audiences returning week after week to catch up with the latest episode, it was a wonderful way for producers to build up the movie habit among the people. In America, the serial queen was Pearl White, whose stardom was

TOP LEFT: Barbara Bedford (left) and William S Hart (right) in Hart's last western, *Tumbleweeds*.

ABOVE: After Hart, the other great cowboy star of the silent era was Tom Mix, seen here (left) in *The Lucky Horseshoe*.

RIGHT: William S Hart in *Hell's Hinges*, typically playing a bad man redeemed by the love of his leading lady.

LEFT: Pearl White (right) in *The Perils of Pauline.*

RIGHT: A publicity still of Pearl White.

FAR RIGHT: A poster for Thomas Ince's *Civilization*, a film that caught the country's (short-lived) pacific mood.

BELOW: Pearl White in one of many fraught situations in *The Perils of Pauline.* The series started a craze among movie-goers and consolidated the movie-going habit.

a pacifist allegory in which the spirit of Christ returned to earth and ultimately triumphed in his quest for world peace. It was a film whose theme was in line with President Wilson's international policy and who is generally thought to have triumphed in the presidential election of 1916 because he had secured his promise of keeping America out of the war. But there were strong contrary voices also being heard. The mood of pacifism had been shaken by the sinking of the *Lusitania* in 1915, in which Americans were numbered among the dead. The fact that it was a victim of a sneak (i.e. 'cowardly') submarine attack added to the feeling of anger. (It might be compared with the mood that followed Japan's surprise attack on Pearl Harbor in 1941, which prompted America's entry into the

established by her serial, THE PERILS OF PAULINE (1914). In France, the fantasy serials of Louis Feuillade, FANTOMAS (1913-14), LES VAMPIRES(1915-16) and JUDEX (1916) acquired a considerable following. In LES VAMPIRES, the French police struggled rather helplessly against the villainous Irma Vep, while JUDEX was rather more conventional in its attitude to law and order, with Judex being a figure of mystery who rights injustices. These films were admired considerably at the time by the Surrealist artists, who loved the movies' visual qualities and particularly the way they made the world of the everyday look increasingly dramatic and mysterious. Feuillade was more or less forgotten by the time of his death in 1925 but was to be rediscovered by film historians. Georges Franju's film, JUDEX (1962) was an attempt to recreate the visual style and moral world of the period. 'In homage to Louis Feuillade', reads Franju's end title, 'in memory of a period that was not happy, 1914-1918'.

How were the movies of the time reflecting that period? What attitudes to the war did they reveal? Politically, America's position was initially non-interventionist, and Hollywood has always been reluctant to lay itself open to accusations that it was trying to influence its country's foreign policy. Significantly, one of the most successful films of the time was Thomas Ince's production, CIVILIZATION (1916),

Second World War.) Also, an overtly propagandist film such as J Stuart Blackton's THE BATTLE CRY OF PEACE (1915) made no bones about its pro-war stance and its blunt tactics in persuading the public about the true nature of the 'enemy'. This movie was to be credited as the first to establish the stereotype of the German officer – militaristic, brutal and bestial – which was to become so prevalent in future American war movies.

In fact, the tide of political and public opinion began to change. As we have seen, D W Griffith's IN-TOLERANCE, which was premiered in September 1916, was not a commercial success. There may have been several reasons for this, but one was undoubtedly that its theme of universal brotherhood struck the wrong chord at the time. Film historians have wondered ever since if the fortunes of that film might have been much better had it only opened a

ABOVE: Alla Nazimova protects her friend in the controversial *War Brides*. This was Nazimova's first film; she went on to cultivate a remote and

beguiling screen image, acting in a highly stylized manner.

RIGHT: A distraught Nazimova in *War Brides*.

few months earlier. Similarly, Herbert Brenon's WAR BRIDES (1916), in which Alla Nazimova played a young factory worker whose husband is killed in the war and who shoots herself rather than allow her unborn child to be born into a warmongering society, had its release suppressed, because it was thought its message might be misunderstood. It was correctly anti-German, but it was also anti-war at a time when such a position was losing its authority and appeal.

ABOVE: Charlie Chaplin in *Shoulder Arms*, experiencing the danger and drudgery of life in the trenches. Even sleep proved difficult, as his bunk bed disappeared under a sea of muddy water.

LEFT: Charlie escaping from the Germans in *Shoulder Arms*.

ABOVE RIGHT: Charlie turns the tables on some German soldiers in *Shoulder Arms*. He will later capture the Kaiser – but it is only a dream . . .

When America entered the war on 5 April 1917, pacifist films were withdrawn and replaced by films whose intentions were clear from their titles: THE KAISER – THE BEAST OF BERLIN, and THE PRUSSIAN CUR, for example. Gradually the whole film community became deeply involved in the war effort. Jesse Lasky and Cecil B De Mille formed the Jesse Lasky Home Guard. German actors in Hollywood were obliged to change their names for the duration of the war. Even the name of sauerkraut was changed to liberty cabbage.

Erich von Stroheim, who was technically a deserter since he was still an Austrian citizen at this time, appeared to relish the situation, playing Prussian villains in films and seeming quite unconcerned when pelted with bread rolls and gravel on stepping out in public. By contrast, Charlie Chaplin was acutely embarrassed by the hostile publicity he attracted through not returning to England for war service (as it happened, he had volunteered but had been turned down on medical grounds). By way of compensation, Chaplin became a tireless campaigner for the sale of US War Bonds and was supported in this by, among others, Douglas Fairbanks and Mary Pickford. Politicians rapidly discovered that the crowds they could attract were miniscule in comparison with those drawn by the stars. After all, the audience had never heard these people speak.

Chaplin made his own war film in 1918, SHOULDER ARMS, with the Tramp as a reluctant soldier enduring the horrors of trench warfare and finally capturing the Kaiser. Like Chaplin's later comedy in 1940, THE GREAT DICTATOR, there was a strong underlying seriousness to the comedy and a danger that it would be regarded in bad taste, but Chaplin's talent prevailed. It was an enormous hit, and probably the only great film about the war to come out during the actual war period. One particularly memorable scene had Chaplin fussing with the making of his bed in the trenches as if he were a hotel maid, and then sinking into it – literally, for he disappeared into the mud. 'I remember how hard I laughed and how sad I felt', said Budd Schulberg. 'That was the measure of his genius'.

Earlier D W Griffith had been commissioned to make a film advancing the Allied cause, and he made an official tour of the Western Front in 1917 with his cameraman Billy Bitzer. As part of the Griffith project the Gish family were also sent to France, a period during which their mother got severely shell

LEFT: Rex Ingram directed *The Four Horsemen of the Apocalypse*, based on Blasco-Ibañez's best-selling novel.

BELOW: Mary Pickford in *The Little American*, Cecil B De Mille's indictment of American neutrality.

RIGHT: The village on the Marne in *The Four Horsemen of the Apocalypse*.

shocked. 'Viewed as a drama', Griffith was to say, 'war is disappointing'. He meant that it had none of the excitement, glamour and heroism of the propaganda: all he saw was what he described as 'the aching desolation of nothingness' and 'soldiers standing up to their hips in ice cold mud'. The resulting film, HEARTS OF THE WORLD (1918), was mostly shot in America and concerned the invasion of a French village by the dastardly Germans. It featured an early film appearance by Noel Coward, and Erich von Stroheim acted as a sort of unofficial technical adviser.

Griffith's sentiment and sensitivity were perhaps a little too sophisticated for audiences at that time. Closer to the national mood were the pro-war films of Cecil B De Mille who invariably, in Joseph L Mankiewicz's inimitable phrase, 'had his finger up the pulse of America'. In JOAN THE WOMAN (1917), an English soldier finds a rusty sword which prompts a dream about Joan of Arc (Geraldine Farrar) and, inspired by her example and patriotism, he leads a

raid on the enemy the next morning. In THE LITTLE AMERICAN (1917), 'America's sweetheart', Mary Pickford, was rescued from rape by the nasty Germans only in the nick of time. The film's blunt statement of its position on the war was reflected in one of the titles: 'Then I stopped being neutral and became a human being'. Audiences responded to the message, but they did not seem to like their sweetheart being put in such danger. An important lesson was learnt here about the star system – the public would not tolerate much deviation from its expectations. Mary Pickford was to remain 'Little Mary' and 'America's sweetheart' to the American public, even when she was old enough to be a grandmother.

The end of the war in 1918 brought an end to the vogue for war films, which, with the exception of Chaplin and Griffith, had generally been of indifferent quality; when their emotional resonances diminished they had very little to recommend them. War movies that had been started before the end of hostilities in Europe were either junked, re-

LEFT: Neil Hamilton and Carol Dempster, with arms raised, in Griffith's last independent production, *Isn't Life Wonderful?*, set in postwar Germany.

RIGHT: Dolores del Rio in *What Prince Glory?*

BOTTOM LEFT: A vividly violent battle scene in *What Prince Glory?*, in which one of the extras was killed. Film-making in those days could be a very hazardous enterprise.

BELOW RIGHT: Pola Negri in *Barbed Wire*.

shot, or shown as planned but now to half empty cinemas. The mood changed. Whereas the European movies of the postwar period inevitably reflected to some degree the pessimism and hardships of the time, America was entering the Jazz Age and the Roaring Twenties, and audiences now wanted to see stories of success.

Nevertheless, there were a number of distinguished films made in the 1920s about the First World War which reflected more humanitarian values now that the need for propaganda against Germany had eased. Rex Ingram's THE FOUR HORSEMEN OF THE APOCALYPSE (1921) had a pacifist message, though is best remembered today for a tango sequence that made a star out of Rudolph Valentino. D W Griffith's ISN'T LIFE WONDERFUL? (1924) was a sympathetic study of life in postwar Germany. Its theme of love conquering all perhaps sentimentalized the portraiture, but Lillian Gish thought it one of Griffith's best movies. Raoul Walsh's WHAT PRICE GLORY? (1926) was more of a study of the cameraderie of men at war and became a huge hit, partly because of its unheard coarse language. 'After the picture ran two or three weeks at the Roxy Theatre', recalled Walsh, 'they got thousands and thousands of letters from lip readers that said it was the most disgusting picture they ever saw, and the most ter-

ABOVE: Action from *Wings*, a hymn to the 'warriors of the sky' of World War One.

LEFT: John Gilbert and Renée Adorée as the reunited lovers in *The Big Parade*.

RIGHT: Clara Bow as a patriotic nurse in *Wings*.

rible language that these men were talking. Now, that also sent people back who saw it. They became lip readers.' In a similarly rugged vein was WINGS (1927), a story of the aerial dog-fights of the Great War entrusted to director William Wellman because he had himself been a combat pilot, and distinguished by some astonishing aerial camerawork. By contrast, Rowland Lee's BARBED WIRE (1927), in which a French girl (Pola Negri) falls in love with a German prisoner-of-war (Clive Brook) exemplified the more conciliatory feelings of the time.

If there was one silent movie about the First World War that towered above the others, it was King Vidor's THE BIG PARADE (1925). Vidor's intention was simply to present the war as seen through the eyes of an ordinary soldier, who was neither a pacifist nor a patriot. Quickly sketching the hero's community and the American attitudes to the war, the film's tone darkened considerably when it moved into the war zone itself. Few films of the time could match it in its evocation of the preciousness of life and love, the fear of death, the common humanity that linked both friend and foe, nor its uncompromising depiction of the suffering wrought by combat. 'No love has ever enthralled me as the making of this picture,' said John Gilbert, who was superb in the leading role. 'It was the high point of my career'. The film made Gilbert a star, and he was soon to rise even higher in the public's eyes as a romantic leading man – for Garbo was beckoning.

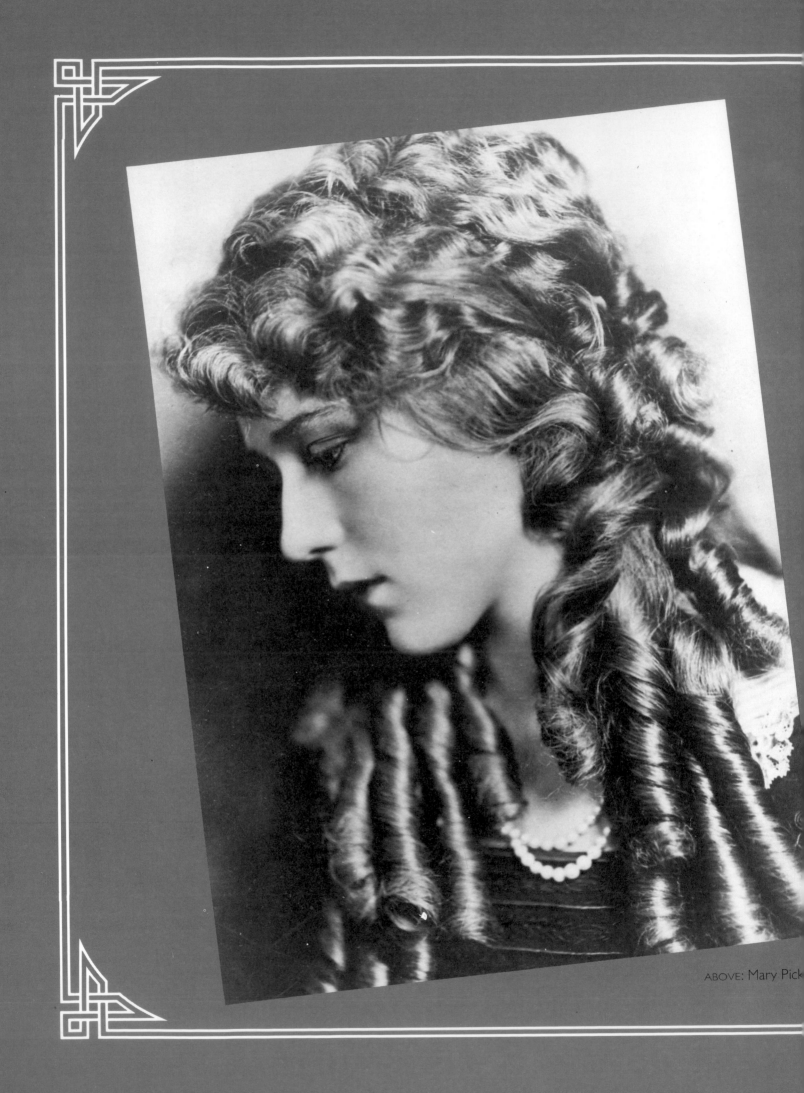

CHAPTER FIVE
Temple of Sex

'The cinema . . . that temple of sex, with its goddesses, its guardians and its victims.' (Jean Cocteau)

Although the star system was not invented by the cinema – for writers, actors, composers had become legendary celebrities a long time before the birth of Hollywood – nevertheless the evolution of the film star was one of the phenomena of the early twentieth century. Film stars in Hollywood became America's royalty. They attracted a quite unprecedented public interest and adulation, but in some cases fame and wealth were bought at a terrible price.

The development of the star had a profound influence on the history of film. It affected the evolution of film technique. For example, there is no doubt that the discovery and development of the close-up and the feature length film were intimately connected to the public's interest in stars. The public wished to see their favorites at close quarters, hence the close-up. They wished to see them in an adventure or story which fully elaborated their personality, hence the development of the feature-length film. Indeed the star also had a considerable effect and impact on the industrial growth and structure of the film industry. During their attempt to gain a monopolistic stranglehold on the film industry, the Motion Picture Patents Company had been reluctant to name the actors and actresses in their movies, in case (as happened in the theater) they became popular and demanded higher salaries. Because the film was regarded as a rather vulgar entertainment at that time, most performers were happy to retain their anonymity. In his book, *A Pictorial History of the Silent Screen*, Daniel Blum quoted a trade journal of 1910 which said that 'while the pictures have attained a distinct prominence and are now recognized as a standard attraction, the people playing in them are very sensitive about having their identity become known. They have an impression that the step from regular stage productions to the scenes before the camera is a backward one'. However, the independent producers shrewdly saw that the star of a film was often its principal selling point, the main reason why an audience came to see it. They began to name their actors and actresses as a matter of policy. It gave them an instant advantage over the product of the Patents Company, who eventually and reluctantly had to follow their example.

A famous publicity stunt organized by one of the shrewdest of the independent producers, Carl Laemmle, set the seal on the emergence of the star. 'We Nail a Lie', proclaimed Laemmle in an advertisement in the magazine *The Motion Picture World*, refuting a purported rumor that the actress known to nickelodeon audiences as the 'Biograph girl' had been killed in a streetcar accident. This was a dastardly plot by the Trust, said Laemmle, to cover up

the fact that the lady in question, Florence Lawrence, had signed up for Laemmle's own company. He neglected to mention that the rumor had actually been started by himself. When he sent Miss Lawrence on a publicity tour to demonstrate that rumors of her death were greatly exaggerated, she was mobbed by enthusiastic crowds. The era of the star was born.

One can gain some idea of the way the power of the star rocketed in a short time simply by surveying the salaries of some of them. Charlie Chaplin went from $150 a week in 1913 to $1,250 a week in 1915, to $10,000 a week in 1916, to a million dollars a film about a year later. At first simply known by the public as 'Little Mary' after a character she played in several films, Mary Pickford became a star on a scale to rival Chaplin. By 1919 'America's sweetheart' was earning more than a million dollars per film.

Mary Pickford, whose real name was Gladys Smith, had been discovered by D W Griffith and established herself in early films for him at Biograph, such as AN ARCADIAN MAID (1910) and WILFUL PEGGY (1912). As her stardom grew, Mary, in harness with her equally ambitious mother, became one of the sharpest business women in America: she may well have been the first self-made millionairess. Stories were told of her stopping at cinemas showing her movies to count how many people were in the audience. As was often remarked by the tycoons who had to deal with her, there was a tough little mind beneath her famous golden curls. Yet to the public she was 'Little Mary' and, in that, was perhaps the first movie actress to embody what was to be a fundamental characteristic of the star: an identification in the public mind between the actual personality of the actor or actress and that of the characters whom he or she played. Could Mary Pickford reconcile this image with her lifestyle? A friend remembered how she agonized over her impending divorce, and her planned marriage to Douglas Fairbanks, 'Will my people ever forgive me?' Mary asked. It was not only the question itself that was significant: it was the way in which the question was phrased, as if she were royalty contemplating abdication. As it happened, it became quite clear that the American public would forgive Mary Pickford anything – even some of her films.

LEFT: America's sweetheart, Mary Pickford as Pollyanna.

companions look suspiciously like Doug Fairbanks and Charlie Chaplin.

BELOW: Mary Pickford as Pollyanna; her buggy

ABOVE: The tomboy with the curls: Mary Pickford in *Little Annie Rooney*. Privately the actress felt she was getting a bit old for this sort of thing.

LEFT: Love in a department store: Mary Pickford in *My Best Girl*, co-starring Charles 'Buddy' Rogers (later to become her husband).

RIGHT; Mary Pickford as Little Annie Rooney, a spunky child coping bravely in adversity.

'She was not just the first screen idol', said B P Schulberg, an executive and producer at Paramount, 'She had become a national institution – the symbol of rags to riches, of the good little girl overcoming evil. The titles of the pictures we made with her say a lot about what she meant to America: CINDERELLA, POOR LITTLE RICH GIRL, POLLYANNA, REBECCA OF SUNNYBROOK FARM, A DAWN OF TOMORROW. I really think she was the perfect symbol of our own wide-eyed innocence, before the war and the new generation of sheiks and flappers changed our morality.' To the list of films cited by Schulberg, one might add other hugely popular Pickford films such as SUDS (1920), where she played a Cockney laundry worker; LITTLE LORD FAUNTLEROY (1921), in which she triumphed in a dual role as Cedric the 'sissy' and his mother; and LITTLE ANNIE ROONEY (1925), an Irish romp in which she was the daughter of a New York cop. Notice the recurrence of the word 'little' in the titles, plainly a calculated remembrance of the 'Little Mary' who first came to prominence – despite the fact that by the time of ANNIE ROONEY, she was thirty-two years old and had been married twice. To the American public she seemed a perennial child.

As previously mentioned, one film that was a comparative failure with the American public was Cecil B De Mille's THE LITTLE AMERICAN, in which Pickford was threatened with rape by German soldiers and played an altogether more mature character than was her custom. The public resisted this attempt to broaden her image. In another movie, STELLA MARIS (1918), she played a dual role which allowed her to present a darker side to her predominant screen image, in the same way that Olivia de Havilland played good and bad identical sisters in THE DARK MIRROR in 1948. This too was unsuccessful. In 1929 she won an Oscar for her performance in her first sound film COQUETTE, in which she appeared with a new hair-style and a jazzy personality to match. But the public remained wedded to her former persona of purity and morality, uncloying charm, resilience and 'apple pie' homeliness. Chaplin was happily able to ring the changes on his image of the 'little fellow', but Mary Pickford remained imprisoned in the image of 'Little Mary' which made her rich but from which she never escaped.

If the American public found the spectacle of their 'sweetheart' in sexual peril in THE LITTLE AMERICAN just too much to take, it is interesting to remember that there was a similar scene in Griffith's HEART OF THE WORLD where the Germans were battering at the door and the hero was prepared to put a bullet through Miss Gish rather than allow her to have to

submit to a fate worse than death. In his book, *The War, the West and the Wilderness*, Kevin Brownlow quoted a contemporary reviewer as saying: 'Mr Griffith is entirely justified in using so old an expedient as the man about to kill the woman he loves; in such a situation it is the right thing to do.' Lillian Gish was perhaps the silent screen's other great example of American purity, a being so ethereal and fragile that she scarcely seemed flesh and blood at all. Even when she was ostensibly cast against type, as the branded adultress in Victor Seastrom's film version of Hawthorne's THE SCARLET LETTER (1926), for example, her innate virtue still shone through – appropriately so, in this particular case. Indeed, some of the most powerful acting in all silent cinema comes from the spectacle of Miss Gish defending her body and soul against brute masculinity and then bearing the consequences: in Griffith's BROKEN BLOSSOMS and in Seastrom's wonderful poetic melodrama, THE WIND (1928).

ABOVE AND LEFT: Lillian Gish, the silent screen's most ethereal heroine and one of its finest actresses, seen here in *The Wind*.

RIGHT: Wedding night; Lillian Gish in Griffith's *Way Down East*. Griffiths once said of her, 'She is not only the best actress in her profession, but she has the best mind of any woman I have ever met.'

LEFT: The vamp: Theda Bara in the title role of *Cleopatra*.

BELOW FAR LEFT: The exotic sensuality of Theda Bara.

BELOW LEFT: The 'It' Girl, Clara Bow.

RIGHT: Clara Bow as an unlikely dusky maiden in *Hula* (1927).

BELOW: The lustrous Louise Brooks.

At the other extreme of this virginal image of woman on screen was the vamp. The first great vamp was Theda Bara, who in reality was a tailor's daughter from Cincinnati, called Theodosia Goodman. Her screen name was an anagram of 'Arab Death'; and her image, as particularly exemplified by her title role in CLEOPATRA (1917), was one of deadly Eastern promise. Her publicity was as lurid as could be imagined, with one particularly famous still of her as she gazed hungrily at a skeleton, by implication all that was left of the poor fellow after the vamp had finished with him. 'Kiss me, my fool!' was a title from A FOOL THERE WAS (1915), which was her first starring role; and the line became something of a catch phrase. She enjoyed playing up to her screen image, being served in public by 'slaves' and often greeting the press while stroking a snake in a room reeking of incense. In a way the image self-destructed, becoming eventually more absurd than alluring. After the war and now moving into the Jazz Age, male audiences seemed to want a more modern image of womanhood. They found it in Clara Bow.

'Clara Bow was the most marvelous star of the twenties because she *was* the twenties', wrote actress Louise Brooks (who herself was to give the silent screen's most subtle and seductive performance of the *femme fatale* as Lulu in the 1929 classic, PANDORA'S BOX). 'Garbo came from Europe, Swanson was already very sophisticated and dressy in De Mille films, but Clara was the real jazz baby.' Bow's biggest hit was IT (1927), written by Elinor Glyn because as she said: 'of all the lovely ladies I've met in Hollywood, Clara Bow has it! . . .' For a brief spell, Clara was known nationally as the 'It' girl. Unfortunately, as one wag noted, when sound came to the movies, she was soon to be known as the 'Ain't' girl.

BELOW: 'She's a ripping sort really; she's absolutely heavy with 'It'!' Clara Bow and William Austin in *It*.

RIGHT AND FAR RIGHT: Publicity stills of Clara Bow. Her popularity soared in 1927, but was short-lived. Malicious rumors about her romantic affairs, and her own physical and mental infirmity all helped to end her career just after the arrival of the talkies.

The career of Clara Bow was to become one of the earliest and most painful examples of the pitfalls of stardom. She was, in a way, the Marilyn Monroe of her age, except that where Marilyn was a sensitive and intelligent woman forced to inhabit the persona of a dumb blonde, Clara Bow was, according to Budd Schulberg, 'an easy winner of the Dumb-bell award', which meant that her fame with the public was also peculiarly mixed with a sense of contempt and feelings of superiority over her. An emotional response from her for a scene could simply be induced by playing 'Rock-a-Bye-Baby' on the set, for it conjured up memories of her early life in Brooklyn. Like Marilyn Monroe, Clara Bow had endured a horrendous childhood, bullied by a drunken, unemployed father and by a violently unstable mother who threatened to kill her if she went into movies. Her break came when she won a beauty contest and the chance of a movie contract, which was her only hope and means of escape from home. Fame struck like lightning, but with the coming of sound, her career suffered a severe reversal that was never to be checked. Because of the necessity in the early days of sound of keeping the camera in sound-proof booths to cover its whirring noise, action was limited and this vital and active actress suddenly found her movements severely restricted. She was also teamed alongside trained theatrical actors like Fredric March and looked amateurish and awkward in such company. Also her stock-in-trade characterization of the flighty and featherbrained flapper-girl suddenly seemed unfashionable and even frivolous in an era that had just seen the Wall Street crash and was moving into the Depression. Scandalous revelations about her private life by a secretary, Daisy De Voe added to her troubles, as did a series of gambling debts. Her career was really over by 1930 and her next 35 years were to be a slow, grim haul towards death, with many stops en route at various sanitoriums. 'Her life,' said Louise Brooks, 'was really as terrible and tragic as actresses such as Joan Crawford love to imagine theirs.'

Joan Crawford rivaled Clara Bow in the 1920s as an incarnation of unzipped femininity, but a stronger erotic glow began to emanate from the repressed, subtle sexuality of Greta Garbo. After the Bows and the Baras, who tended to flaunt their sexuality with all the finesse of a fly-swatter, Garbo offered an altogether more sophisticated version of the *femme fatale*. There was an element of neurosis about her, reminiscent of Nazimova. An aura of doom clung to her like a shroud: she was the only female star, it was said, who could die at the end of her movies and be assured of public approval. Like Valentino, she was incomparable at suggesting the excitement and mystery of sex, but behind that, her romanticism

was not exotic but melancholy, with a sense of exhaustion, hidden suffering and noble stoicism.

Born in Stockholm in 1905, the daughter of a peasant laborer, Garbo had worked in a barber's shop as a lather girl before finding employment as a film extra. Her real name was Greta Gustafsson, but it was changed to 'Garbo' – the Swedish for 'wood sprite' – when she was discovered by the great Swedish director Mauritz Stiller, who gave her the lead role in his film, THE ATONEMENT OF GOSTA BERLING (1924) and became her mentor and father figure. When Louis B Mayer offered Stiller a contract to direct films in Hollywood for MGM, he brought Garbo with him. Ironically, Stiller could not adjust to Hollywood methods of working and returned to Sweden in 1927, dying there a year later. By contrast, Garbo was an instant sensation.

After her first Hollywood film, THE TORRENT (1926), she was soon teamed with a sympathetic cameraman, William Daniels, who was to photo-

LEFT: Greta Garbo, shortly before her arrival in Hollywood. with the look of enigmatic beauty that made her famous.

RIGHT: Garbo in her first great screen success, *The Atonement of Gosta Berling.*

LEFT: Incandescent passion: John Gilbert and Greta Garbo in *Woman of Affairs*.

RIGHT: Gilbert and Garbo in their first film together, *Flesh and the Devil*.

BELOW RIGHT: Gilbert and Garbo in their last film together, the talkie *Queen Christina* (1933). Garbo's popularity expanded with the coming of sound, but Gilbert was one of its most notable casualties.

graph all but four of her movies, and achieved her greatest success in the silent era when co-starred with a romantic leading man, John Gilbert, in FLESH AND THE DEVIL (1927) and LOVE (1927), a version of Tolstoy's ANNE KARENINA. As with the Elizabeth Taylor-Richard Burton films of more recent times, the public seemed to gain an extra voyeuristic *frisson* from the spectacle of an on-screen romance that, according to rumor, was continued off-screen as well. The famous scene where Gilbert lights Garbo's cigarette in FLESH AND THE DEVIL seemed to ignite visible sexual sparks. In life, Gilbert was to be deserted by Garbo at the altar and become one of the sound era's most celebrated tragic sacrifices, not so much because of his supposedly high-pitched voice, but because of the atrocious dialogue he was given as the screen's great lover. (In his first talkie, HIS GLORIOUS NIGHT, his first line was: 'O beauteous maiden, my arms are waiting to enfold you.') Unlike Gilbert, Garbo made a triumphant transition to the sound era. Somehow, as she continued to play women torn either by passion or by the struggle for

survival in a man-made world, her deep, thickly accented voice seemed entirely appropriate to her world-weary image. Further, unlike many who attempted to straddle the sound era through stridency, Garbo seemed instinctively to recognize the secret of screen acting: that quality of inwardness, where acting is less important than reacting.

Nevertheless, the most popular screen actress of the 1920s was undoubtedly Gloria Swanson. Elinor Glyn described her as 'the new kind of woman – daring, provocative, sensuous'. Early in her career she had made romantic comedies for Mack Sennett, but her fame particularly spread after a series of films with Cecil B De Mille, like DON'T CHANGE YOUR HUSBAND (1919) and MALE AND FEMALE (1919) in which she flirted wittily with sexual themes while keeping both feet on the ground. In 1922 one of Swanson's directors (and later one of her husbands), Marshall Neilan wrote an article entitled 'Acting for the Screen' in which he listed what in his view were the six great essentials: beauty, personality, charm, temperament, style, and the ability to wear clothes. Of

LEFT: The silent screen's most glorious clotheshorse: Gloria Swanson.

BELOW: Thomas Meighen and Gloria Swanson in *Male and Female*.

RIGHT: Elegance personified: Gloria Swanson. A born showwoman she was well aware of the value of publicity, and every move she made received full press coverage.

LEFT: Gloria Swanson as Sadie Thompson, the fallen woman of Somerset Maugham's notorious play, *Rain*.

ABOVE: Sadie in reflective pose. Swanson received an Oscar nomination for this role.

all actresses during that decade, Swanson was the one, above all others, who had the lot. She was also a shrewd and ambitious woman who was not afraid to take risks. Sometimes the risks paid off, as with her decision to make a film version of Somerset Maugham's notorious *Rain*, entitled SADIE THOMPSON (1928), during what could be most charitably called a period of moral timorousness in the history of the movies. Sometimes the risk failed, as with her project directed by Erich von Stroheim, QUEEN KELLY (1928), which she halted in mid production. (It is the film she and William Holden are watching in *Sunset Boulevard*, quoted at the beginning of this book). She took it all in her stride as part of her recognition of how movies and the star system at that time worked. 'If I succeeded', she said, 'they (i.e. her co-stars, the crew etc.) would all succeed richly

because of me. If I failed, the failure would be mine alone; and they could all move on to something else'. Such was the egotism, and the responsibility, of the star at the time. Swanson might have boasted, but she did not exaggerate.

One of Swanson's successes of the early 1920s was BEYOND THE ROCKS (1922), in which she played an aristocratic young lady who is married off to an elderly millionaire, but who falls in love on her honeymoon with a dashing young man who sweeps her off her feet with a tango. The rising young co-star was Rudolph Valentino. If Swanson was the most popular actress of the 1920s, Valentino was the silent screen's most charismatic leading man. He was born Rodolfo Guglielmi in Italy in 1895 and inherited his dancing skills from his mother (his father was an army veterinary surgeon). By all accounts he had been a reserved and rather morose child, often getting into trouble with his father for missing school. The faint scar on his cheek, which Hollywood publicity elevated into a dueling wound, had actually been caused by his father's razor.

At the age of 18, Valentino had emigrated to America, where he stayed with an Italian family and learnt English. During this time he had jobs as dish-

LEFT: On the set of the ill-fated *Queen Kelly*, Gloria Swanson chats to her (third) husband, Marquis Henri de la Falaise.

RIGHT: Rudolph Valentino in *The Four Horsemen of the Apocalypse*.

BELOW: The famous tango scene in *Four Horsemen*: Valentino with Helena Domingues.

washer, messenger and garbage collector, before being employed as a professional dancing partner (a euphemism for gigolo) in a fashionable New York club called Maxim's. In 1917 he decided to try his luck as an actor in Los Angeles. Spotted by Dorothy Gish, who thought he had star potential, he almost landed a leading role in Griffith's SCARLET DAYS (1919), but the part finally went to Richard Barthelmess. The break came two years later with his role in THE FOUR HORSEMEN OF THE APOCALYPSE, but the film in which he literally made women faint in the aisles was THE SHEIK (1921).

It was THE SHEIK which established the prototype of the Valentino mystique: that of an exotic, alien man who threatens sexual ravishment but who also promises untold illicit pleasure. Although dubbed 'The Latin Lover', Valentino seemed at his most romantic when playing an Arab, and some have wondered whether the contemporary tales of Lawrence of Arabia rubbed off on to Valentino, flavoring adventurism with the spice of eroticism. The publicity was the most lurid and ludicrous since Theda Bara: 'Shriek for the Sheik will seek you too!' The visual symbolism used to reinforce Valentino's image of virility – spiky spurs, bullet-loaded belts etc., – was hardly any more subtle. He personified sleek sexuality, and was the forerunner of such stars as Ramon Novarro and Gilbert Roland.

The most immediately striking thing about Valentino's image was that it appealed infinitely more to women than to men. If he served as a stimulator of female fantasy, he was the subject of some vicious articles by men, particularly an attack in the *Chicago Tribune* in 1926, who described men who imitated Valentino's style of behavior as 'pink powder puffs'. (According to David Shipman in his valuable study of eroticism in the cinema, *Caught in the Act*, this was 'because a dance-hall had installed in the men's room a machine emitting face powder for its clients' powder puffs, apparently because of Valentino's influence') Valentino's sensuality seemed to stimulate only the envy and xenophobia of the average American male, and it was not until the appearance of Clark Gable in the 1930s that Hollywood discovered a truly all-American romantic hero who appealed to both men and women.

In the case of Valentino, the contrast between his persona on screen and his personality off screen could not have been more extreme. If Clara Bow could be seen as a sort of silent cinema forerunner of Monroe, Valentino was its Elvis Presley: instinctively erotic in performance, but quite withdrawn, and even diffident away from the public gaze. His power over women on screen was overwhelming. Yet in his private life he was dominated by women. He married the starlet Jean Acker, who sued him for bigamy when he divorced and remarried within a year, an unknowing violation of Californian law. His second wife was Natasha Rambova (real name: Winifred Hudnut), who was a company heiress and part of a Hollywood lesbian set headed by Nazimova. Both ladies were immensely strong willed; in both cases the marriages were unconsummated and both women seemed to have used the marriage to further their careers. A costume and set designer who became a sort of unofficial and uninvited producer on Valentino's films, Rambova alienated the other technicians and studio heads. She did steer Valentino to one of his biggest successes in BLOOD AND SAND (1922), but her interference was beginning to be injurious to Valentino's career. At this time, the American writer H L Mencken was describing Valentino as 'a gentleman in an intolerable situation'. Quite contrary to his screen image, Valentino was a weak personality held in thrall by women whom he viewed as sexual aggressors.

Whether Valentino's acting style would have survived the transition to Talkies is a moot point. 'My God, those flapping nostrils', commented the critic Gordon Gow, and even Adolph Zukor, no mean student of the histrionic art, had to concede that Valentino's acting was largely confined to 'protrud-

LEFT: Latin lover with Eastern spice: Rudolph Valentino in *Son of the Sheik*. By the time this movie was released in 1926, Valentino was being lambasted in the press as a 'painted pansy', but this still didn't diminish his appeal to women.

RIGHT: Rudolph Valentino and Vilma Banky in *Son of the Sheik*.

ing his large, almost occult eyes until the vast areas of white were visible, drawing back the lips of his wide mouth to bare his gleaming teeth – and flaring his nostrils'. By contrast, his fellow actor John Gilbert called him 'a prince of gallantry. Beyond all his many other attributes of artistry, comeliness and charm, a gift of royal bearing lent glamor to his being, which made him the hero-lover of all time'. What clinched Valentino's immortality – as it would Monroe's, Presley's and James Dean's – was his premature death.

Rudolph Valentino died in 1926 from the combined effects of acute appendicitis and a gastric ulcer. His death triggered the biggest display of mass hysteria over a film star ever witnessed. The actress Pola Negri embraced his coffin, a proprietorial gesture and probable publicity stunt that lost her legions of fans overnight: this was too serious for mere displays of grief, for many women took his death deeply to heart. Some took poison, others threw themselves off skyscrapers, and still others shot themselves before shrines set up in his honor. Billy Wilder's SOME LIKE IT HOT (1959) alludes to this period when Sweet Sue's Society Syncopaters are looking for their usual female replacement for their all-girls band. Says the agent sadly: 'She slashed her wrists when Valentino died'.

The mass morbidity over Valentino's death was one striking manifestation during the decade of the public's fascination with the film star. Another was public reaction to a series of scandals that rocked Hollywood in the early 1920s. One of them was the reaction to the unsolved murder in 1922 of William Desmond Taylor, a sophisticated and distinguished director of some Mary Pickford vehicles and adaptations of such wholesome American classics as TOM SAWYER (1917), ANNE OF GREEN GABLES (1919) and HUCKLEBERRY FINN (1920). The author, Sidney Kirkpatrick has recently told the whole story in his book, *A Cast of Killers*, and it would be unfair to reveal his solution to the mystery. Suffice to say that revelations which followed about Taylor's drug-taking and unconventional, not to say unacceptable, sex life implicated the actresses Mabel Normand and Mary Miles Minter who had visited him on the night of the murder. It effectively ended the career of Mary Miles Minter, who had been one of the silent screen's most popular child stars and whose image was as snow white as Mary Pickford's. 'Without doubt she was the best looking youngster I ever saw', said director Edward Sloman, adding 'and the lousiest actress'. A harsh judgment and not entirely fair, but there was no doubt her career had been thriving prior to the discovery of her dubious relationship with Taylor. Mabel Normand was simply one of the most talented comediennes in films, but the Taylor scandal, followed shortly after by another

in which her chauffeur shot a millionaire at a party of Edna Purviance's with a gun owned by Miss Normand, finished her career completely. She died of pneumonia and tuberculosis in 1930.

The Taylor scandal was followed by the death in 1923 of the actor Wallace Reid of morphine addiction. Reid was a tragic case for his addiction had started when he had been injured on location during the making of the film VALLEY OF THE GIANTS (1919) and had been given a massive injection of morphine to enable him to get through the film. His wife, the actress Dorothy Davenport was to star in an anti-drugs film the following year, HUMAN WRECKAGE (1924) to highlight the folly and tragedy of drug addiction.

The most notorious scandal, however, involved the trial of Fatty Arbuckle for the alleged rape and murder of a young actress, Virginia Rappe, after a party at the St Francis Hotel, San Francisco on 5 September 1921. Arbuckle was tried three times, with the juries on the first two occasions failing to agree on a verdict. The third jury not only acquitted Arbuckle but augmented their verdict with a fulsome apology that asserted he was not only innocent and free from all blame but that a great injustice had been done in bringing him to trial in the first place. Nevertheless, during the trials the studios had been increasingly nervous about public reaction and threatened with dismissal any employee who wished to testify as a friend on Arbuckle's behalf. Despite the jury's verdict, Arbuckle was banned from the screen.

It is perhaps not too difficult to understand now why these scandals made such an impact, though at the time the film community was completely taken aback by the storm of protest. It was rapidly found that scandal involving movie stars did more for newspaper sales than any other subject or theme, so the press milked the stories for all they were worth and were not to be expected to show restraint or discretion. The attitude of the public was also one that perhaps we recognize more readily now than they would have done then: a disgust and fascination intensified by their jealousy and envy of stars, who seemed to have everything in the way of money and glamour and yet still could not behave decently.

The Arbuckle scandal 'had drawn the lightning on us all', said Gloria Swanson. Stars were compelled to sign studio press releases extolling the married state, often while in the midst of negotiating their own divorce. They were forced to sign a contract with a morals clause, which gave the studio the right to end the contract immediately if the actor or actress 'was charged with adulterous conduct or immoral relations' with men or women other than their husbands or wives. For Gloria Swanson, the pressure of this morals clause was later to compel her to have an abortion, for the birth of a baby out of wedlock would have meant the end of her career and financial ruin. It was a decision, she said, that she regretted for the rest of her life. Because she had

played the Madonna in Cecil B De Mille's KING OF KINGS (1927), the actress Dorothy Cumming could not get her desired divorce until what was deemed the end of the life of the film – in this case seven years – because her contract for the film stipulated that 'she must observe and act in entire accord with strict Christian conduct and behavior'.

Hollywood in general, and De Mille in particular, were not slow in figuring ways round these restrictions, paying lip-service to morality while giving the public a high old sensual time. 'A rash of Bible pictures solved the fornication problem for the major studios', said screenwriter Ben Hecht. 'Immorality, perversion, infidelity, cannibalism etc., are unassailable if you dress them up in the togas of the Good Book'. Nevertheless, something seismic had happened during that period, which was to affect Hollywood in the future. The star had been made aware that, if stardom had its perks, it also had its penalties. Hollywood had come to realize that it was on safest ground when it appealed squarely to the morals of middle America. This suggested a popular direction for the future. However, whether it would add up to more exciting, challenging movie making was another matter.

ABOVE LEFT: Valentino in *Blood and Sand*, a story of passion and the bullring, co-starring Nita Naldi.

RIGHT: Rudolph Valentino in *The Young Rajah* (1922).

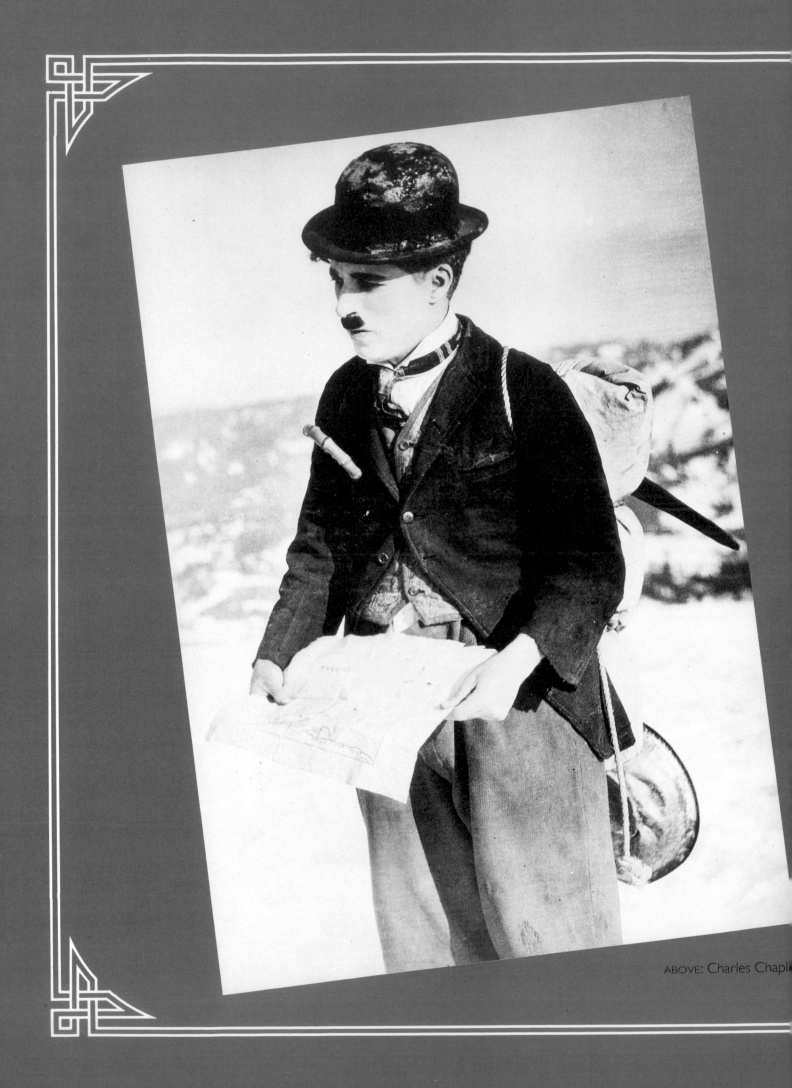

ABOVE: Charles Chapl

CHAPTER SIX

Buster and The Tramp

'Truth is the first essential of comedy'. (Charlie
Chaplin)

In the house of a stone-faced comedian in 1920, his guest, the world's most revered tramp, was holding forth about politics. 'What I want', cried Charlie Chaplin, pounding the table for emphasis, 'is that every child should have enough to eat, shoes on his feet and a roof over his head!'

'But Charlie', replied Buster Keaton, quietly, 'do you know anyone who doesn't want that?'

There is a touching innocence about both attitudes, but it is an exchange that in some ways crystallizes the difference between the images and personalities of the two men. Chaplin was the angry sentimentalist, whereas Keaton was the more matter-of-fact stoic. Nowadays it has become fashionable to deride Chaplin for his simple, heart-on-sleeve philosophizing in his comedies and to prefer Keaton's less tearful, more tenacious refusal to submit to his fate. This is probably an inevitable reaction against the unprecedented adulation afforded to Chaplin during his lifetime, albeit alternating with periods of vicious vituperation that would have felled lesser men; and a reaction in a cynical century against Chaplin's naked emotion. Keaton's soaring reputation after his death is also part compensation for the neglect he endured after the coming of sound. Even Buster, who was not a bitter man, had to say about his rediscovery in the early 1960s that: 'It's come about thirty years too late'. Still, whatever the respective merits or demerits of Chaplin and Keaton, the current critical sport of elevating one at the expense of the other seems not only pointless but positively ungrateful. Why make do with one genius when you can have two? Together they comprise the twin glories of silent film comedy, enriching it equally from radically different standpoints.

'Like myself', said Keaton, 'Charlie was hit by a make-up towel almost before he was out of diapers'. By the time both stepped in front of a camera for the first time they had accumulated a wealth of comic business, material and technique from their experience in music-hall and vaudeville. Both had made their stage debuts by the time they were five, but, in both cases, these early stage appearances were peculiarly mixed up with the domestic situation in their households: the young Buster being knocked around on stage by his increasingly alcoholic father; Chaplin's debut being a warmly applauded parody of his mother who had just been booed off the stage. The proximity between knockabout comedy and real-life cruelty was probably subconsciously apparent to them both from an early age. Keaton's childhood has been held responsible for some of his psychological problems in later years, notably his passivity and his alcoholism, whilst Chaplin's childhood could be said to hold the

LEFT: Peering through the tent: Chaplin in *The Circus*, for which he won an honorary Oscar.

RIGHT: Two of life's strays: Chaplin and Scraps in *A Dog's Life*.

key to his entire personality and work.

The life of Charlie (or, as he was later to become, Sir Charles Spencer) Chaplin is the most extraordinary rags-to-riches story of the twentieth century. He was born in London in 1889, the son of two minor music-hall performers. His father deserted his mother when Chaplin was a child and died an alcoholic when the boy was twelve. His mother was a manic depressive who suffered a severe mental breakdown which led to her confinement in a workhouse asylum for long periods. With his elder brother Sydney, Chaplin spent much of his early life in a Victorian poor-house. It is tempting to see the women in Chaplin's subsequent films as a reflection of the elusive beauty of his mother whom he idolized, but for whom he also probably cherished a feeling of resentment. 'Her only crime, motherhood', is a famous title from THE KID (1921); in THE GREAT DICTATOR (1940), he was to give the

heroine his mother's name, Hannah, and end the film on a close-up of her face, and on the words: 'Lift up your eyes, Hannah. Look toward heaven, Hannah, can you hear me? Listen!' With his background it is not surprising that he fixed on the Tramp as his comic persona, and that his films were to be full of references to poverty and hunger.

Chaplin's performing gifts soon gained him recognition and he became a star attraction of Fred Karno's famous pantomime troupe. On one of their American tours his 'Night in an English Music Hall' act was spotted, allegedly by Mack Sennett himself, who certainly had an eye for talent and who at that time needed a replacement comedian for Ford Sterling in case Sterling carried out his threat of leaving Keystone. Chaplin was signed up by Keystone Studios in 1913 and soon made his screen debut in MAKING A LIVING (1914), but for a while he wondered whether he had made a mistake. The money had

been a powerful attraction, but Chaplin preferred live theater to film and really wanted to do drama rather than comedy. His main anxiety was his feeling that his own comedy style did not fit in with Sennett's. Chaplin's derived from character, while Sennett's depended on the chase. 'Must every comedy end on a chase?' Charlie asked forlornly.

Legend has it that the Tramp came into being one afternoon when Chaplin was mulling over his dissatisfaction with his screen work and rummaging around Sennett's costume department, looking for a distinctive outfit that would set him apart from the other members of Sennett's team. He came across a pair of outsize trousers, a derby hat, a tight coat, a cane, a pair of floppy shoes, and a little brush-like mustache. One other feature was added: a shuffling splay-footed walk that he copied from an old pedlar he remembered seeing as a child on the London streets, who walked that way because his shoes were too small but who could not afford another pair.

From the moment that the Tramp first appeared on screen in 1914 (Chaplin's autobiography says its was MABEL'S STRANGE PREDICAMENT but it was actually in KID AUTO RACES AT VENICE), he was a sensation, quickly becoming, in the critic David Robinson's phrase, 'the most universally recognized fictional figure ever created'.

Chaplin was later to elaborate on the significance and meaning of the costume. The derby, he said, stood for dignity; the mustache represented vanity; the coat, stick and manner were a gesture toward gallantry, dash and front. The whole was a personification of shabby gentility. The character thought of himself not so much as a Tramp as an aristocrat who had fallen on hard times. 'This fellow is many-sided,' Chaplin would say, 'a tramp, a gentleman, a poet, a dreamer, a lonely fellow, always hopeful of romance and adventure. He would have you believe he is a scientist, a musician, a duke, a polo player. However, he's not above picking up a cigarette butt,

RIGHT: Comedy of objects: *The Pawnshop*.

RIGHT: Comedy of objects: *The Pawnshop*.

LEFT: The Tramp tries to sneak an abandoned baby into a vacant pram in *The Kid*. This was his first feature-length film and was hailed as a masterpiece.

or robbing a baby of its candy'. Part of the pathos and complexity of the character comes from the split between what he is and what he imagines himself to be; and between what he desires and what society allows. The essence of the Tramp's comedy, Chaplin thought, lay in the character's concept of his own dignity, which he clung to as desperately as he hung on to his shabby trousers. The Tramp was someone who 'having had something funny happen to him, refuses to admit that anything out of the way has happened and attempts to maintain his dignity.... All my pictures are built around the idea of getting me into trouble and so giving me the chance to be desperately serious in my attempt to appear as a normal little gentleman', said Chaplin. Given the stress on dignity, it was not surprising that the main targets of the Tramp's humor were those social figures of pomp and authority who tend to stand on ceremony: the wealthy, the aristocratic, the enforcers of the law.

Many arguments have been put forward about the basis of the Tramp's phenomenal appeal. For the critic James Agee, the Tramp was as multi-faceted a character as Hamlet, a universal figure who exemplified what the human being is capable of, and up against. For Federico Fellini, the Tramp 'was a sort of Adam, from whom we are all descended... There were two aspects of his personality: the vagabond, but also the solitary aristocrat, the prophet, the priest and the poet'. François Truffaut put it most simply. 'Without willing it or knowing it', he said, 'Chaplin helped men live'. Truffaut was thinking particularly of the period when the Tramp first appeared on the screen. At that time in America there was widespread malnutrition, poverty, vagrancy and appalling housing, particularly among the large immigrant population. For the working classes of that time, the only relief and affordable entertainment were the movies. The Tramp became their Everyman, and his vulgarity, which horrified

LEFT: A drunken Charlie fights a losing battle with his bed in *One A.M.*

FAR RIGHT: Chaplin as a cop bringing law and justice to the slums in *Easy Street*.

BELOW: Repairing – or rather demolishing – the watch in *The Pawnshop*.

some polite audiences, only made him all the more endearing and special. He made people laugh and forget their troubles, but he did more than that: he gave them hope. The Tramp might be downtrodden but he was also defiant. He could be roughed up but he was resilient, a resourceful David against the Goliath of modern times.

Without needing to be told, audiences sensed an emotional authenticity in Chaplin's portrayal of the Tramp. This was not simply someone acting like a Tramp, using the clothes as a sort of unfancy dress. Somehow audiences felt that this was someone who knew what it was like not to know where the next meal was coming from, who knew something about that life from the inside. This is not to forget the Tramp's comedy nor to underestimate Chaplin's phenomenal mastery of mime and movement, but it was undoubtedly the additional human dimension of the character that lifted Chaplin above his other comedy rivals at that stage. By one of those characteristic showbiz paradoxes, the Tramp was to make Chaplin a millionaire, but even at the height of his popularity, Chaplin would say: 'I've known humiliation. And humiliation is a thing you never forget. Poverty – the degradation and hopelessness of it! I can't feel myself any different at heart from the unhappy and defeated men, the failures'.

Chaplin's career in silent movies divided into several distinct phases, as, like all the major moviemakers of the time, he made the transition from one- and two-reelers to feature-length films. Among his best films for Sennett's Keystone Company were THE MASQUERADER (1914), where he turned up in female disguise (one of a number of his early transvestite performances) and LAUGHING GAS (1914), where he caused chaos as a dental assistant. Moving to another film company, Essanay, in 1915, at ten times the salary Sennett had originally paid him, Chaplin made 14 films during that year. THE TRAMP (1915) was especially popular, and ended in a manner that was to become something of a Chaplin trademark: the long walk of the Tramp away from the camera along a lonely road into an uncertain future. Another particularly popular short of this time was THE BANK (1915), in which Charlie played a janitor in love with a typist and who dreams of being a romantic hero, only to wake up and find himself kissing a mop. Dream sequences were to become important in his films, sometimes comic but often as a sort of safety valve at a point of crisis, like the Tramp's dream of paradise when he seems to have reached a dead end in THE KID.

Moving to the Mutual Company in 1916, Chaplin was quickly to make four of the finest shorts of his career. THE PAWNSHOP (1916) is famous for its celebrated scene where the Tramp demolishes a clock

he is supposed to be expertly inspecting and repairing. Although Chaplin professed not to like ONE AM (1916), perhaps because he felt it a mechanical elaboration of a situation rather than an exploration of character, it contained some of his most inspired slapstick as a drunkard's return home turns into a nightmarish encounter with stuffed animals, sliding rugs, a viciously swinging pendulum and a recalcitrant bed. In EASY STREET (1916) the Tramp became a policeman, and Chaplin introduced a vein of social satire which was to become ever stronger in his movies.

THE IMMIGRANT (1916) deserves a special mention, not only because it was a superb comedy, but because it contained the single most astounding shot in Chaplin's entire career, one that has since been quoted in contexts as diverse as Terence Malick's glowing period drama, DAYS OF HEAVEN (1978) and Louis Malle's autobiographical wartime reminiscence, AU REVOIR LES ENFANTS (1987). As they ecstatically get their first glimpse of the Statue of Liberty, the Tramp and his fellow immigrants suddenly find themselves roped in like cattle by unsympathetic customs officials. To this day, nobody has questioned the symbolism of America's famous Statue as forcefully as that. With hindsight, this scene seems chillingly prophetic of Chaplin's later difficulties with the American authorities who questioned his political views, and even of the sequence of events which led him to choose exile in Switzerland in 1952 rather than go through the humiliation of having to apply for a visa to re-enter a country in which he had lived for nearly 40 years. Yet at the time of THE IMMIGRANT, it is certain that the shot had a completely different meaning for Chaplin. As the critic Isabel Quigly commented, the film seemed simply to highlight the outcast aspect of the Tramp's nature: 'The Tramp is an eternal outsider to ordinary society, the immigrant an outsider compared with the native, and Chaplin himself was not merely an immigrant in America, but an immigrant in the entire society to which, with success, he had suddenly climbed. For a climber, however much welcomed, never belongs. . .'

As Chaplin began to assume more and more control of his career, new dimensions of pathos and courage came into his work alongside the comedy. As well as comically criticizing the Kaiser, SHOULDER ARMS (1918) evoked the terrors of the trenches. THE PILGRIM (1923), in which he played a convict disguised as a minister, was not afraid to ridicule America's religious rural community. In THE KID (1921), the Tramp found himself looking after an abandoned child (the astonishingly gifted four-year-old Jackie Coogan) in a relationship in which the Tramp found himself playing Fagin to the kid's Artful Dodger. Yet it included tears along with the laughter, and a stinging attack on the insensitive and callous way the administrators of society treat the unfortunate within its midst. One remarkable scene showed the Tramp in pursuit across a rooftop of an official car that is taking the kid away to an orphanage. It is one of the most original chase sequences of silent cinema, but the accent was not on comedy and slapstick but on sentiment and suspense. In this scene Chaplin was emulating not Sennett but Griffith, and the reunion occasioned not delighted laughter, but tearful joy.

ABOVE: Welcome to America: immigrants stare at the Statue of Liberty just before being roped off like cattle. Chaplin, Edna Purviance (center) and Kitty Bradbury in *The Immigrant*.

RIGHT: Chaplin and Jackie Coogan in *The Kid*, with the omnipresent threat of the law behind them.

FAR LEFT: An escaped convict disguises himself as a preacher: Chaplin in *The Pilgrim*.

In 1923 Chaplin made the most unusual and controversial of his silent movies, the feature length A WOMAN OF PARIS (1923), starring his favorite actress of that time, Edna Purviance. Chaplin got the idea for the film from a meeting with Peggy Hopkins Joyce, who had graduated from being a barber's daughter and Ziegfeld girl to being, at different times, the wife of five millionaires. Chaplin himself only appeared in a brief walk-on part as a railway porter. (It is sometimes said that this brief walk-on was the inspiration for Hitchcock's idea of making short personal appearances in his films.) Conceived as a Hardyesque drama of fate, the plot concerned a country girl (Purviance) who, deserted by her fiancé, travels to Paris and is seduced by the glamour and corruption of the city. She becomes the lover of a suave playboy (Adolphe Menjou) but, when her former fiancé reappears and is subsequently killed defending her honor, she repents and returns to the country with her fiancé's mother. The playboy subsequently

passes her on the road without seeing her and, in a final conversation with a friend, seems barely able to remember her. The film was far ahead of its time in the complexity of its characterization; the harshness of its social comedy (like the moment when socialite heroine petulantly throws her jewelery out of the window and then rushes downstairs to retrieve it from a bemused tramp who could not believe his luck); and, particularly, in its sexual frankness (Menjou's status as the woman's lover is discreetly but unmistakeably signaled in his taking a pair of his cufflinks from the woman's drawer).

A WOMAN OF PARIS was not a popular success, Chaplin meeting the kind of audience resistance that was in later years to plague Woody Allen when he attempted to move into the realm of serious drama. But it had an important impact on Chaplin's peers and fellow film-makers. Ernst Lubitsch, who was to become one of the screen's masters of the sophisticated adult sex comedy, confessed himself overwhelmed by the film and its influence on his subsequent work was very strong. Eisenstein thought it was the cinema's major achievement up to that time. 'I reckoned that if the film was capable of that sort of subtlety,' said the young Michael Powell, who was to become one of Britain's greatest film makers, 'it was the medium for me'. The film remained unseen for many years until, shortly before his death in 1977, Chaplin composed a new musical soundtrack for its re-release. It emerged anew as one of the great films of the silent era.

LEFT: Edna Purviance (left) and Chaplin in *Work* (1915).

RIGHT: Adolphe Menjou and Edna Purviance in *A Woman of Paris*.

BELOW: Chaplin directing *The Gold Rush* in Truckee where the incident of cannibalism, that gave Chaplin the idea for the film, originally took place.

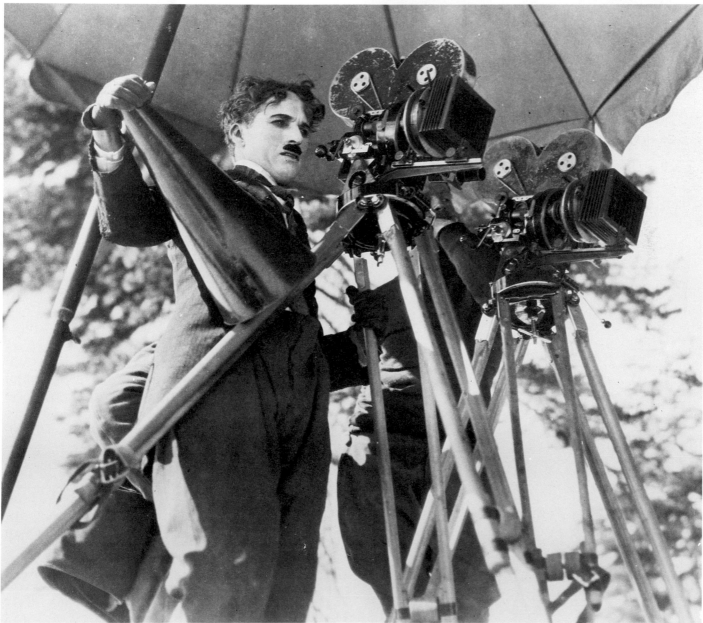

LEFT: Chaplin in *The Gold Rush* in which hunger and greed were the main themes.

BOTTOM LEFT: Practice makes imperfect: Charlie learns the trade in *The Circus*.

RIGHT: Merna Kennedy and Chaplin in The Circus.

The public, however, was clamoring for the return of the Tramp and what followed was THE GOLD RUSH (1925), one of the greatest and most popular of Chaplin's comedies and his own personal favorite. The Tramp this time was a prospector in the Klondike, beset by misfortune and rejection, inevitably falling in love but less predictably, having to avoid being eaten alive by a crazy starved miner who thinks the Tramp is a chicken. The film's themes of starvation and cannibalism, not to mention greed and madness, could hardly have been more savage and desperate, yet they seem to have inspired Chaplin to new heights of comic invention. The famous dance of the rolls, improvised by the Tramp when he is waiting in vain for the heroine (Georgia Hale) to appear and share his feast, was actually a routine originally performed by Fatty Arbuckle in THE COOK, but fits the context of Chaplin's film very well, as the Tramp absent-mindedly tries to kill time. Vintage Chaplin are the scenes in which his cabin almost totters over the edge of a crevice, and in which he has to make a meal out of his own stewed boots to stave off hunger. Chaplin suffered for his art, for the bootlaces were made of liquorice and he was so sick after filming the scene that he had to cancel the next day's shooting. The scene remains as the quintessence of Chaplin's performing art and of the Tramp's character, as the Tramp sets about this gruesome grub with all the finicky finesse of a galloping gourmet, determined to find something sustaining out of some-

thing appalling through sheer will of the imagination.

For 'versatility and genius in writing, acting, directing and producing THE CIRCUS (1928)', Chaplin was awarded a special Oscar. Ironically, it is not one of his best films and Chaplin neglected even to mention it in his autobiography, perhaps because its making coincided with a period of great personal unhappiness when he was suffering from severe nervous strain and going through his second divorce. The film boasted some fine set pieces, where the Tramp, who has been taken on by a circus after interrupting a performance and causing more

mirth than the official acts, found himself locked in a cage with a sleeping lion, or was assailed on a tightrope by some escaping monkeys. One particularly skillful sequence created comedy from the Tramp's unsuccessful attempts to be funny as a clown. Yet the film was essentially episodic and seemed clouded by Chaplin's doleful mood at the time, never more so than in the famous finale, where the circus packs up its tent and departs, leaving the Tramp alone amongst the debris in a deserted field. It was one of Chaplin's most forlorn images of the Tramp – an outcast at life's feast.

When Chaplin was asked what he thought of

Talkies he was characteristically blunt. 'I loathe them', he said. For the first ten years of the sound era he resisted cinema's latest innovation and, although they had music and sound effects added, CITY LIGHTS (1931) and MODERN TIMES (1936) were in essence silent movies, and also among Chaplin's finest and most successful. In MODERN TIMES Chaplin tantalized his audiences with talk of a kind – the Tramp sang a nonsense song in a language that one critic dubbed as 'desperanto' – and finally, at the end of THE GREAT DICTATOR (1940), Chaplin burst forth into a torrent of words as his hero articulated a credo that had previously been implicit in the Tramp's whole progress: 'More than machinery we need humanity. More than cleverness, we need kindness and gentle-

ness'. In later years, he was to be vilified for his private life (his four marriages and a scandalous paternity suit filed by the actress Joan Barry) and hounded out of America for his socialist and pacifist political views during the period of McCarthyist witch-hunts and Cold War. Although there is some dispute about Chaplin's post-Second World War work – for this writer, MONSIEUR VERDOUX (1947) is an unqualified masterpiece, and even the patchy A KING IN NEW YORK (1957) is a political satire of considerable courage and integrity – it undoubtedly never matched the popularity of his silent period work. The Tramp strolled into the sunset at the end of MODERN TIMES never to return, but also never to be forgotten.

RIGHT: Multiple Buster Keatons in *The Playhouse*. This was a surrealistic short filled with shots from Keaton's vaudeville past and some memorable photographic effects.

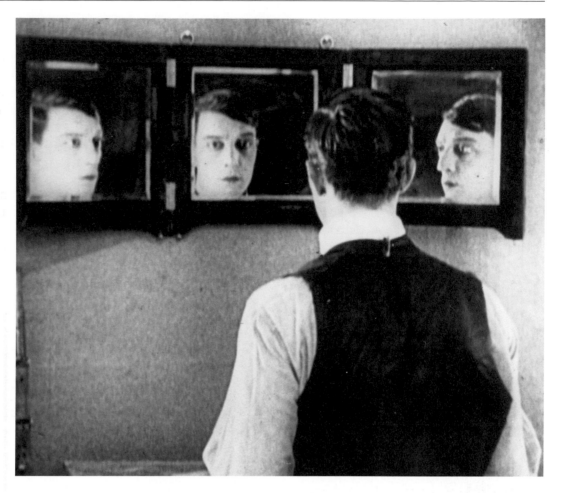

LEFT: Charlie with the drunken millionaire (Harry Myers) whom he has saved from suicide in *City Lights*.

If Chaplin's reputation receded in the sound era, Buster Keaton's well nigh disappeared. It was a curious irony that some of Keaton's early sound films for MGM were more commercially successful than his silent features like THE GENERAL (1926), which lost money. Yet the movies were so poor and forgettable that one would have to be a Keaton connoisseur even to name them. His creative decline in the first decade of sound has been attributed to many causes, both personal (his alcoholism, his broken marriage to Natalie Talmadge) and professional (his supposedly monotonous speaking voice, his loss of creative control over his assignments). When sound came, Keaton thought he had the solution: why not leave him silent, and let the sound go on all around him? But nobody listened. Perhaps Keaton's period had truly passed. For one thing, as James Agee said, 'he was by his whole style and nature so much the most deeply "silent" of the silent comedians that even a smile was as deafeningly out of key as a yell'. For another, it would have been miraculous if Keaton could have sustained the invention he showed between, for example, 1923 and 1928, a period during which he made 12 features to Chaplin's three and where his achievement indisputably outshone that of the man Keaton himself described as The Master.

Born Joseph Francis Keaton in 1895, Buster

acquired his nickname when he was six months old, after falling down a flight of stairs but emerging completely unscathed. 'That's some buster your baby took', said his godfather, the escape artist Harry Houdini, and the name stuck. His ability to fall gracefully was demonstrated even more spectacularly at the age of three, when a cyclone lifted him out of a hotel room. The town was almost totally flattened but baby Buster landed on his bottom four blocks away completely unhurt. The incident might well have inspired one of his most amazing visual gags – because it was not faked – when a housefront is blown down on top of Buster during a tornado in STEAMBOAT BILL JR. (1928) but he survives because a window frame at the top of the house passes harmlessly over his body. Buster joined the family act, the Three Keatons, at the age of four. His act consisted mainly of being knocked around on stage by his father; alternatively, his father would literally sweep the floor with Buster's outstretched body. What such treatment did to his psyche is impossible to gauge, but it certainly taught him how to fall. Buster was soon an accomplished acrobat and, when his father's alcoholic state made it difficult for the act to continue in its original form, Buster took over and began to establish a considerable reputation in vaudeville.

There is some dispute over how Buster came to

meet Fatty Arbuckle. One story is that he literally bumped into Arbuckle walking along Broadway, and Arbuckle, who had seen Keaton's stage work, asked if he were interested in doing movies. 'Come down to the studio Monday', he said to Buster, 'and do a scene or two with me and see how you like it...' He rapidly became Arbuckle's protegé. Keaton's first camera appearance in THE BUTCHER BOY (1917) was shot without rehearsal in one take, an almost unheard of occurrence for a newcomer. Even at that stage, Buster was a natural, which might be one reason why recognition of his genius was so long delayed: he made everything seem so effortless that the painstaking rehearsal to make it appear that way was overlooked. Arbuckle was to direct Keaton in a number of shorts before Arbuckle joined Paramount in 1919 and Joseph Schenck set up a new company to produce Keaton shorts. It should be noted that Keaton was one of the few to stand by his friend when the 'Arbuckle Scandal' broke, paying part of his salary to Arbuckle until the latter's death in 1933 and securing him work as a director under the pseudonym of William B Goodrich. (Keaton's

suggestion for a name had been 'Will B Good'.)

Even by the standards of the comedy classics of Sennett, Chaplin and Lloyd, Keaton's short films, made between 1920 and 1923, still look quite exceptional. ONE WEEK (1920) concerned Buster's attempt to assemble a house using a 'do-it-yourself' package he had received as a wedding present. His jealous arch-rival had mixed up all the parts, and the door ends up on the second floor. Later, finding he has built it in the wrong spot, Buster tries to move all the stuff and gets stuck on a railway line with a train approaching. Amazingly, it veers off on to another track, and Buster and wife are just about to celebrate when their house is crushed by a train coming from the opposite direction. The film's comic ingenuity was breathtaking. The only reservations were of a kind that were to recur in criticisms of Keaton's work: a feeling that the gags were so clever that they inspired admiration more than amusement (Chaplin seemed a little more human, more down-to-earth); and a sense that the underlying tone of the films was somewhat sombre.

A similar feeling permeated COPS (1922), a film in

LEFT: In *Sherlock Jr*, Buster Keaton plays a cinema projectionist who dreams himself into the film he is projecting.

RIGHT: Keaton and Kathryn McGuire in *The Navigator*, Keaton's biggest commercial success.

ABOVE: Buster Keaton alone at the altar in *Seven Chances*. He must marry to inherit a fortune: as word gets out, he is not alone for long.

LEFT: Buster takes a fall in *Battling Butler*.

RIGHT: Buster aims to milk Brown Eyes in *Go West*.

which an innocent Buster became caught up in an anarchist's plot and found himself being pursued by a city's entire police force – a state of affairs precipitated by his failure with the girl he loved. Behind the comedy one could read it almost as a Kafkaesque vision of Man pursued by the Law, by Fate. Technically it was supreme, particularly one superb shot where Keaton, with his back to the camera and facing an approaching army of cops, grabbed on to the back of a taxi that was moving from left to right in the frame and was whisked away from danger. A brilliant escape, but also an inventive technical device to move to the next scene: Keaton as horizontal wipe.

Keaton's most technically adventurous short was THE PLAYHOUSE (1921), in which every face in the opening scene, whether it be performers, musicians, or audience, was Keaton's. He said he intended a satire on Thomas Ince, who was always claiming credit for every aspect of his films, and he accomplished the effect through a use of multiple exposures. Keaton was always interested in special effects, as was to be shown also in a stunning sequence in SHERLOCK JR. (1924), where Keaton, as a film projectionist, dreamt himself into the movie he was showing and then found himself threatened by rapid montage which kept shifting the surface of his world from under his feet. Whereas Chaplin was a relatively conservative director, using the camera mainly to service his own performance (his basic rule for direction was simply long shot for comedy, close up for tragedy), Keaton was much more adventurous visually and technically, and one of the major directors of 1920s American cinema.

From 1923 Keaton started making full-length comedies and astonishingly, made a dozen in the next five years. His first, THREE AGES (1923) – was, as he candidly admitted, basically three short films stuck together, though the idea was certainly an amusing one: Keaton's version of INTOLERANCE, telling three thematically linked stories at different times in history – Stone Age, Roman, and Modern. His first major feature was OUR HOSPITALITY (1923), in which he played the scapegoat in a family feud. Once again dark forces of social chaos were at work, but the film was chiefly memorable for a beautifully shot long train journey – a sort of rehearsal for THE GENERAL (1926) – and for one of Keaton's most hilarious yet hair-raising stunts, where he swung across a waterfall to rescue a heroine about to plunge to her death below. In THE NAVIGATOR (1924), which was one of Keaton's biggest successes, he rang an infinite number of changes on the situation of two people aboard a deserted ocean liner, bumping into each other, trying to make an intimate breakfast in an infinite kitchen, and finally encountering cannibals.

Again this seemed a clever feature-length expansion of a good idea that Keaton had developed in one of his shorts, THE BOAT (1921), in which Buster assembled a boat piece by piece in his basement, unfortunately demolishing his house in the process. The boat is then launched, and instantly sinks, with the only thing left above water being Buster's impervious boater.

In SEVEN CHANCES (1925), Buster played a man who stood to inherit a fortune if he could manage to get married that day. After helpful friends have put an ad in the paper, Buster is besieged by willing would-be brides and the film concluded with one of his most exhilarating comic chases, a device he favored much more than Chaplin did. If BATTLING BUTLER (1926) struck some critics as too sadistic to be really funny (Buster poses as the brutal boxer of the title, but then the real Butler shows up, with violent consequences), GO WEST (1925) struck some others as downright melancholy. Buster's only real friend in this film was a cow called Brown Eyes. When the two go into town, they are followed by a huge herd of amiable cattle. The townspeople, from tap dancers to barbers, panic; a stampede threatens; and Buster rescues the situation by luring the cattle back while wearing a devil's costume. Perhaps because of the simplicity of the structure and because Keaton was always a wonderful actor with animals, GO WEST, if not the most brilliant of the comedies, was one of the most likeable.

Keaton's own favorite of his films and now generally acknowledged to be his masterpiece, was THE GENERAL (1926). It is THE BIRTH OF A NATION of screen comedy and indeed probably more than that: the finest film ever about the Civil War. As well as the humor generated from the central situation – Buster's girl has been captured by Northerners and he pursues her behind enemy lines on his beloved engine, 'The General' – the film was remarkable for its visuals. Keaton wanted it to look like 'a page out of history'. The action revolved around the two classic Keaton situations of a challenge and a chase, in which the hero must redeem himself in the eyes of

the girl he loves; and everything built toward an awe-inspiring shot of the Northern train in pursuit as it falls through the bridge into the water. For obvious reasons, it was a shot that could only be done once, and was reputed to be the most expensive single take of the silent cinema. Crowning the achievement was his own performance; his mistakenly described 'stone face' was actually a map of expressive emotion – concentration, concern and courage. Keaton's essential seriousness of performance derived from an early recognition that the more earnest he appeared, the more laughs he seemed to get. When asked once why he never smiled, Keaton replied simply: 'I had other ways of showing I was happy'.

After COLLEGE (1927), a slight but charming campus comedy in the style of Harold Lloyd, Keaton made STEAMBOAT BILL JR. which, notwithstanding its terrific tornado sequence, essentially seemed a reprise and summation of typical Keaton themes and situations: family rivalry, conflict between father and son, old versus new, and a contrast between modest and macho manhood in which Buster asserts his superiority through resourcefulness more than

ABOVE: The Civil War formed the background of Keaton's personal favorite of his films, *The General.*

RIGHT: Buster tends his beloved engine in *The General.* It is a well-executed film with excellent photography, and the whole production remains effective to this day.

LEFT: Buster, Brown Eyes and stampeding cattle bring city life to a standstill in *Go West.*

ABOVE: Combining duty with pleasure: Buster Keaton and Marian Mack in *The General*.

LEFT: Keaton (left) as Steamboat Bill Jr; Ernest Torrence (right) as Steamboat Bill.

RIGHT: A storm brewing in *Steamboat Bill Jr*.

strength. In retrospect, it seemed as if Buster had come to the end of a particular phase of his career. Indeed he had, for he was embarking on a move which he was later to describe as 'the biggest mistake of my life' – namely, giving up his own studio to sign a contract with MGM. Keaton was freely to concede he was nowhere near as shrewd in his business affairs as were Chaplin and Harold Lloyd, and after two early films THE CAMERAMAN (1928) and SPITE MARRIAGE (1929), which were uneven but had flashes of vintage Keaton, his career was to go into steep decline. It was not to be rescued until James Agee's 'Comedy's Greatest Era' article stimulated renewed interest in his work. He made a potent brief appearance as one of Gloria Swanson's bridge partners in Billy Wilder's SUNSET BOULEVARD (1950) and had an even greater success in a cameo role in Chaplin's LIMELIGHT (1952), where he and Chaplin gave a violin and piano recital so maladroit that they ended up in the orchestra pit. Some said that Chaplin cut Keaton's contribution because it was so good that he feared it upstaged his own performance. However, as the routine came at the end of a long film, it might be that Chaplin's motives were ones of simple dramatic good sense. Also it was suspected that Keaton was underpaid for his significant contribution to the film, though when this point was put to Keaton himself, he replied, with characteristic dignity: 'I would have worked with Chaplin for nothing'. A rather atrocious biopic THE BUSTER KEATON STORY, with Donald O'Connor as Keaton, was made in 1957, which at least gave him financial security for the rest of his life; and his final film

appearance was in A FUNNY THING HAPPENED ON THE WAY TO THE FORUM (1966), directed by one of his greatest admirers, director, Richard Lester.

Comparisons between Chaplin and Keaton will inevitably still be made. Like Chaplin, Keaton was a perfectionist but knew the rules and routines of comedy from a lifetime's experience as a practitioner. Chaplin would rehearse on film (a very expensive practice) to get what he wanted, while Keaton would prepare in meticulous detail in order to try and accomplish what he wanted in a single take: in some cases of course, like the falling of the train through the bridge in THE GENERAL, or the collapse of the house in STEAMBOAT BILL JR., a second take would have been impossible. Like Chaplin, Keaton was essentially a loner both on the screen and off, a mysterious and elusive personality who let few people get close to him. If Chaplin was arguably the more versatile performer with a larger range, Keaton was a better director, with a keener visual style and a wonderful instinct for where to put the camera, to allow space enough in which the character could move. For Paul Gallico, Keaton was 'Frustration's Mime, pursued, put upon, persecuted by humans as well as objects, suddenly possessed of a malevolent life and will of their own'. For George Bernard Shaw, Chaplin was simply 'the only genius developed in motion pictures'. They were more than the screen's supreme comedians. Keaton gave fatalism a new nobility and Chaplin gave humanism a new grandeur. An infant art form that could throw forth two such artists in its first two decades of development was clearly not just lucky, but blessed.

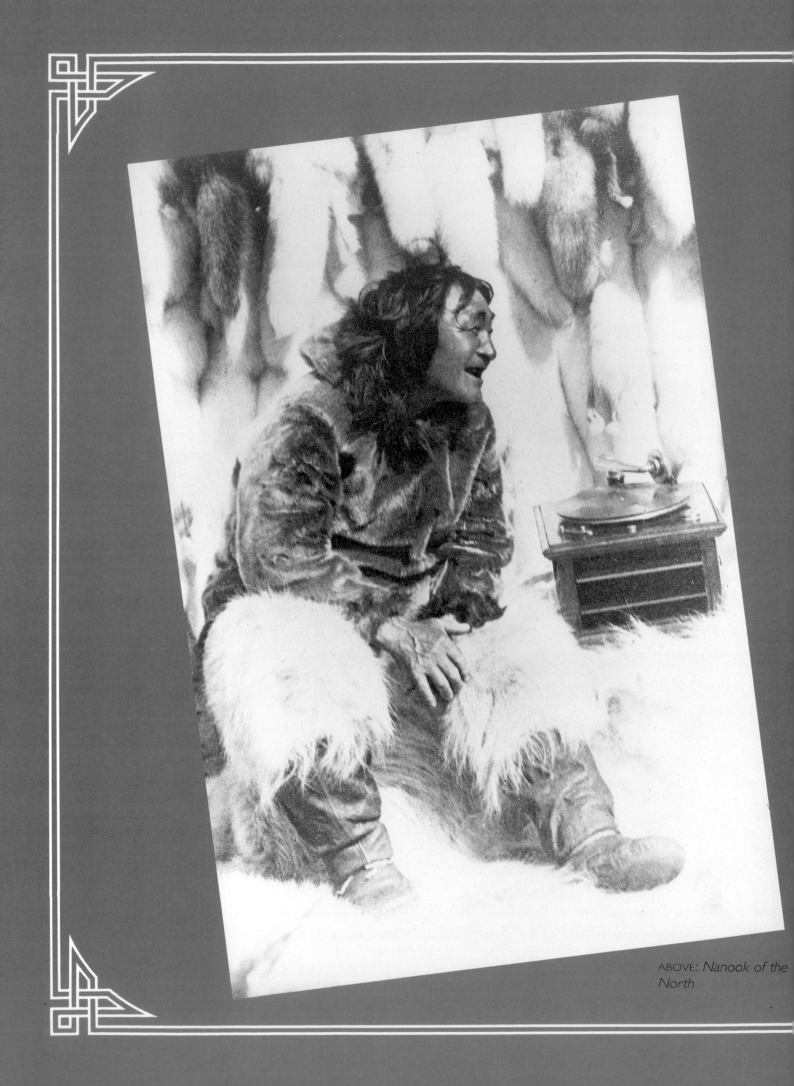

ABOVE: *Nanook of the North*

CHAPTER SEVEN

The Mechanical Eye

'The camera is, in a measure, both the discoverer
of an unknown world and the rediscoverer of a lost
one.' (John Grierson)

From the time of its inception and the pioneering work of Lumière and Méliès, the film industry seemed to be torn between two tendencies: its capacity to copy nature, to photograph external reality as it passed in front of the camera lens; or its ability to create its own fantasy world, to project its audience into an imaginary adventure. This in turn generated large questions about the cinema. How could it be a creative form if it merely reflected the real world? On the other hand, how could it be taken seriously if all it offered was a form of escapism?

These questions increased in urgency as the film developed into a medium of mass entertainment. For the entrepreneurs film was basically an industry, in the business of making a profit. For the artists, film provided, in the words of Erich von Stroheim, 'the greatest means of artistic expression', principally because, more than any other art form, 'you can show life as it is'. Some of the greatest movies of the silent era sought to comment and reflect on the real world and dramatize the problems of ordinary people, appealing to audiences by showing them a heightened reflection of their own lives.

In the early days of the cinema, of course, much of its novelty came from its ability to show people events they had never witnessed before and, in the ordinary run of things, might never have expected to see: the Oxford and Cambridge boat race, the Derby, the coronation of Czar Nicolas II, Queen Victoria's Diamond Jubilee, Scott nearing the Antarctic, even the last hours of Leo Tolstoy as he languished in that station waiting room and refused to allow his wife to see him. The film camera became the most immediate and most trusted of news reporters. 'The Biograph camera does not lie...' claimed *Leslie's Weekly* on 6 January 1900, when it was reporting on the Boer War and the Boxer Rebellion in China, neglecting to mention that many newsreels of the time were faked and action artificially set up for the benefit of the camera. But at this time film conferred authenticity: the camera could not lie.

It should be remembered too, that the film camera opened up a whole new world for some audiences. For many, it was literally the first time in which they had the opportunity to see the inside of a rich person's home, how it was furnished and decorated. The film camera also opened up the world of travel for people. The early travelogues of Martin and Osa Johnson, particularly CANNIBALS OF THE SOUTH SEAS (1912), were very successful, and had a considerable impact on one man who was to become one of the most original of all film makers, Robert Flaherty.

Born in Michigan in 1884, Flaherty in his youth had been a miner, gold prospector, engineer and explorer. Between 1910 and 1916 he had been searching for iron ore on behalf of Sir William Mackenzie along territory around Hudson Bay occupied by Eskimos, with whom he had become very friendly. On one expedition he had taken a motion picture camera to make a film of Eskimo life which he thought might be of some commercial value and which would therefore help offset some of the cost of the explorations. 'While editing the material', Flaherty recounted later, 'I had the misfortune of losing it all by fire'. What had happened actually was that he had inadvertently dropped his cigarette on the film which then went up in flames. In trying to save it, Flaherty had only succeeded in getting himself hospitalized with burns. Far from being a misfortune, it proved to be the turning-point of Flaherty's life. Previously he had been filming as an explorer and geologist but, he said, 'new forms of travel film were coming out and the Johnson South Sea Island film particularly seemed to me to be an example of what might be done. I began to believe that a good film depicting the Eskimo and his fight for existence might well be worth while.... I decided to go North again – this time wholly for the purpose of making films.'

Looking again at the one surviving print of his original film, Flaherty felt that his concept had been entirely wrong. It seemed to invite questions about what he had seen and done when really he had wanted to show the Eskimos, and to show them not from the civilized point of view, but as they saw themselves. 'I realized then', said Flaherty 'I must go to work in an entirely different way'. He decided to take a typical Eskimo and his family and make a biography of a year or so of their lives. After considerable difficulty in finding money he was financed by a firm of fur dealers, Revillon Frères; as his chief character he selected Nanook, 'a character famous in the country', said Flaherty. He was soon to be famous throughout the world. To everyone's surprise, NANOOK OF THE NORTH (1922) was a huge commercial as well as critical success.

The events of the film were ostensibly more mundane than melodramatic, but they caught the popular imagination because of the film's unique vision and its uncovering of a kind of life never before seen on the screen. The action included a seal-hunt and a ferocious struggle with a walrus, the tiger of the North. Family life was sketched in tenderly, and there was some amusing visual observation, such as the moment when Nanook in some curiosity, tried to nibble a gramophone record. (Flaherty was to recall that although the Eskimos seemed to enjoy his records of Harry Lauder and jazz, Caruso as well as Pagliacci was to reduce them to helpless laughter.) The success was totally unexpected because the film

ABOVE: Nanook the hunter in *Nanook of the North*.

RIGHT: The eskimo family of Nanook.

LEFT: Life as dance: the Samoan islanders in *Moana*.

TOP RIGHT: 'The Man You Love to Hate': Erich von Stroheim in *Foolish Wives*.

BOTTOM RIGHT: Intimations of decadence from Stroheim's *The Merry Widow*.

was totally unconventional. It had the slightest of narratives and was a film about a people not just an individual – moreover, a people outside society.

'I want you to go off somewhere and make me another *Nanook*', wrote Jesse Lasky of Paramount to Flaherty. 'Go where you will. Do what you like. I'll foot the bills. The world's your oyster.' In fact, Flaherty went to the islands of Samoa and made MOANA (1926), a film as different in style from NANOOK as the people themselves differed from the Eskimos: hence the film's emphasis on beauty, ceremony and dance rather than, as in the earlier film, on survival. Despite Paramount's hopeful advertising campaign for the film ('The Love Life of a South Sea Siren'), the movie was not a success, but in reviewing it, John Grierson remarked that it had 'documentary value'. It was one of the first occasions that the word 'documentary' had been used about film, and it was to lead to Flaherty being described as the 'father of the documentary film', a title he was later to take pains to disclaim.

Grierson later criticized Flaherty for the absence of political and economic dimensions in his movies, but it was apparent that Flaherty disregarded these simply because they formed no part of his purpose. Flaherty approached cinema not as politician or economist, but as poet and explorer. He was to make films that were hymns to vanishing ways of

life, about elemental struggles for survival, and full of the wonders and terrors of nature and the heroic struggle of humanity for survival. If Flaherty used the camera as an explorer, seeking out lost or hidden worlds, other film-makers of the time used it as a conscience, bringing to the surface social injustices which might previously have remained buried. Victor Sjöstrom's INGEBORG HOLM (1913) was an early example of the social problem film, telling the story of a woman, who, reduced to poverty by the death of her husband and the failure of their grocery business, has to accept incarceration in a workhouse in order to save her children from a life of begging. When her son is seriously ill, she escapes to see him, only to be recaptured and returned; and later she becomes insane when, on a visit, one of her daughters no longer recognize her. The film's impression of life under the poor law made considerable impact, simultaneously compelling politicians to review the kind of conditions which could bring about such a situation, and raising film in the estimation of many critics who had previously thought it offered only diversion or sensation. For better or for worse, realism on the screen was one of the chief ways in which the cinema could get itself taken more seriously. Artists of the caliber of Sjöstrom and Chaplin seemed to demonstrate films could not only be a window on the world, it could also possess a soul. But when did the real become the morbid, or even the sordid?

'By God, I told them the truth', said Erich von Stroheim about his classic, GREED (1923). 'They liked it, or they didn't like it. What had that to do with me?' Few directors took realism (meaning, in this case, the more seamy side of life) to the lengths of Stroheim. For him it meant authenticity of setting, which often involved the expense of filming on location. It meant realism of style which, in his eyes, meant as far as possible the seeing of the action in a continuous flow with as little manipulative montage as possible. Above all it meant the depiction of 'real life', as he called it, 'with its degradation, baseness, violence, sensuality, and, a singular contrast in the midst of this filth, purity'. Stroheim was convinced that, after the war, the public was tired of what he called 'chocolate eclair' cinema, 'Pollyanna stories with doll-like heroines and lily-white heroes'. He was a graduate of Griffith, he declared, and intended to go one better than the Master as regards realism.

Having emigrated to America from Austria around 1910, Stroheim had swiftly assumed the hauteur of Austrian aristocracy, although he was actually the son of a Jewish hatter in Vienna. The impression of nobility was heightened by his imperious manner and by his recurrent theme of the love of a noble-

man for a commoner, which surfaced in such films as MERRY GO ROUND (1922), and THE WEDDING MARCH (1927). His setting was often that of prewar Vienna; the passions were invariably depraved and adulterous; and, from BLIND HUSBANDS in 1919, to QUEEN KELLY in 1928, he anatomized the emotions of military men and monarchs in their death throes. Comparing his work with that of Ernst Lubitsch, Stroheim remarked: 'Lubitsch shows you first the King on his throne, then as he is in his bedroom. I show you the King first in his bedroom so you'll know just what he is when you see him on his throne'.

What characterized Stroheim's style was his uncompromisingly honest depiction of human corruption, and his fanatical attention to detail. It was to lead to Gloria Swanson's cancelation of QUEEN KELLY, when Stroheim seemed to be taking the brothel scenes in Africa to censorable levels of realism. He had also fallen foul of boy-wonder producer Irving Thalberg on MERRY GO ROUND, when Stroheim had spent days rehearsing his cast on parade

procedure and had insisted that even what the cast wore under their costumes should be absolutely authentic to the period. Stroheim was removed from the film. He was to suffer again from Thalberg's interference on GREED (1923), Stroheim's greatest film and the highpoint of realism in silent American film.

GREED was based on Frank Norris's novel, *McTeague*, which Stroheim had apparently read when an impoverished dishwasher in New York. He had even slept with it under his pillow. It told the story of a dentist, McTeague, whose relationship with his best friend Marcus is strained when he becomes engaged to Marcus's former girlfriend, Trina. What changes them all is Trina winning $5,000 in a lottery. She becomes a miser, McTeague a drunken bully who will murder his wife for money, and Marcus an envious fop who will betray McTeague. The two former friends meet finally in a murderous confrontation in Death Valley. Stroheim's filming of the tale was immediately characterized by an emphasis on realism. As far as possible, he filmed on

the actual locations in San Francisco described in the novel. He commandeered blocks of houses, even tearing some down so he could film interiors. He did a month's filming in Death Valley, which put the actors in hospital. Above all, he insisted on filming the novel page by page. He finished with 42 reels of film, which if projected in their entirety, would have run for around ten hours. Unfortunately for Stroheim during the making of GREED, the Goldwyn company merged with Metro to become MGM, which brought him under the control of Louis B Mayer and Irving Thalberg. Describing Stroheim as a 'footage fetishist', Thalberg insisted that the film be cut down from 42 reels to ten. Stroheim was to describe the final result as a 'mutilated child'.

Even in its mutilated form, GREED still looks like one of the milestones of silent film. For Stroheim realism did not preclude symbolism and imagination. He experimented with color to suggest the corruption of the characters by money, having gold painted in on some prints of the film – on the birdcage, on the gleaming knobs on the bedposts.

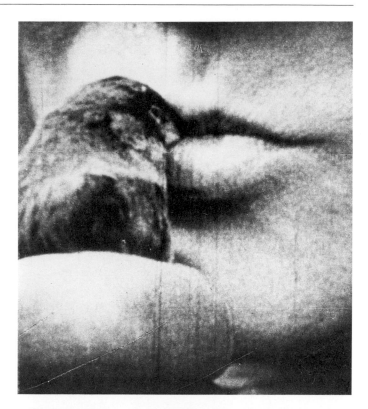

FAR LEFT: Stroheim (right) and Norman Kerry (left) as the Count discuss a scene in *Merry-Go-Round*.

LEFT: Walter Byron and Gloria Swanson in Stroheim's *Queen Kelly*.

TOP: Birds of a feather: *Greed*.

ABOVE: A violent quarrel in *Greed* between McTeague (Gibson Gowland) and his wife (Zasu Pitts).

ABOVE: Murder and madness in the aptly named Death Valley in *Greed*.

TOP RIGHT: From left to right, George K Arthur, Bruce Guerin, Otto Matiesen and Georgia Hale in *The Salvation Hunters*.

LEFT: The wedding feast in *Greed*.

BOTTOM RIGHT: The volatile director Josef von Sternberg.

Typically he showed the extremes of life side by side: a wedding reception, during which a funeral procession passes by the window; a murder scene framed by Christmas tinsel; a desert scene, in which McTeague's money will become as much of a dead weight attachment as the corpse of his friend and where the aridity of the setting seems to be making its own comment on materialist obsession. 'He was the director of directors', said John Grierson of Stroheim, admiring beyond measure his perfectionism, his attention to detail, his disregard of financiers in the pursuit of filmic truth. Directing him as an actor in FIVE GRAVES TO CAIRO (1943) and later, in the immortal SUNSET BOULEVARD (1950), Billy Wilder was to say to Stroheim: 'You were ten years ahead of your time'. With that air of aristocratic arrogance that never left him, Stroheim snapped back: 'No – twenty'.

One young director particularly inspired by Stroheim was Josef von Sternberg, who was to make three silent films in a downbeat realist mode, THE SALVATION HUNTERS (1925), UNDERWORLD (1927) and THE DOCKS OF NEW YORK (1928), which were partially

ABOVE: Evelyn Brent as 'Feathers' McCoy in Sternberg's *Underworld*.

TOP RIGHT: Marlene Dietrich performs and Sternberg directs on the set of *The Blue Angel*.

LEFT: Betty Compson (left) and George Bancroft (right) converse in *The Docks of New York*.

BOTTOM RIGHT: Clive Brook as 'Rolls Royce' in *Underworld*.

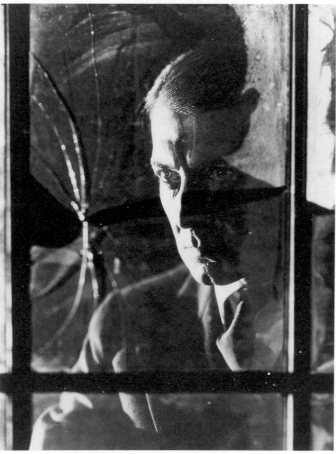

influenced by Stroheim's example. Sternberg was no more a genuine 'von' than Stroheim, and in fact, the backgrounds of the two men were remarkably similar. They were both Viennese from poor families, with a fascination for low life that, in both cases was intensified by a similar love for the naturalistic novels of Emile Zola, which dealt (some say sordidly) with passion, fate and heredity among the lower classes. Like Stroheim, Sternberg was little interested in the commercial movie conventions of plot and heroism. Indeed, UNDERWORLD turned out to be a big hit because of the refreshing way it upturned the conventions. 'The thing to do', said the writer on the film, Ben Hecht, 'was to skip the heroes and heroines, to write a movie containing only villains and bawds. I would not have to tell any lies then'. In the 1930s, Sternberg was to begin his famous series of films with Marlene Dietrich, from THE BLUE ANGEL (1930) to THE DEVIL IS A WOMAN (1935), which had their fair share of decadence and sexual obsession but where the real world was displaced by metaphoric sound stages of dream and desire. It was the birth of a poet, but the death of a realist. 'When a director dies', said the ever-literal John Grierson of Sternberg, 'he becomes a photographer'.

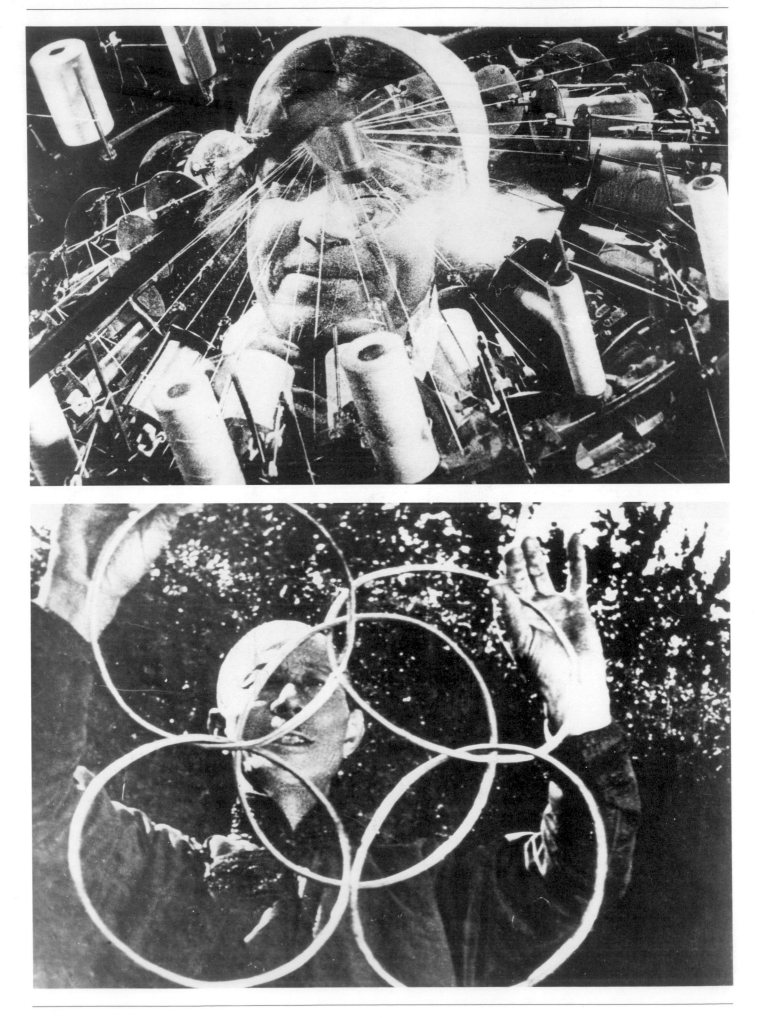

RIGHT: *The Man with a Movie Camera*, Vertov's best-known production.

LEFT: Mesmerizing montage from *The Man with a Movie Camera*, a film about the art of making films.

BOTTOM LEFT: Wheels within wheels: *The Man with a Movie Camera*.

The relationship between photography and realism was given particularly sophisticated consideration by the film theorist and director, Dziga Vertov, who was one of the key figures of Soviet cinema in the 1920s. Like Flaherty and John Grierson, Vertov thought that film could do more than tell stories and that its proper subject should not be fantasy heroes and heroines but, as he put it, 'life as it is'. 'Down with the immortal kings and queens of the screen!' exclaimed Vertov. 'Long live ordinary mortal people, captured in the midst of life, going about their daily tasks... Down with the scripting of life: film is unawares, just as we are'. He was the first great Soviet documentarist, and he described the movie camera as 'a mechanical eye'. However, the great thing about the movie camera, he believed, was that not only was it a mechanical eye, it was a mechanical 'I': in his words, 'I, the machine, show you a world the way only I can see it'. Indeed, the camera could not only reveal someone's subjective vision of the world. Through editing, super-imposition, dissolves etc., the camera could go beyond the potentialities of human sight and capture what the naked eye could not see. All this came together in Vertov's remarkable film, THE MAN WITH A MOVIE CAMERA (1929). This was not only a film of a cameraman's record of city life on an ordinary day, but it also included shots of the cameraman himself taking the pictures, of the editor editing the film, of the audience watching the film in the cinema. It was an extraordinary demonstration of the power of the camera but also the complex relationship between film and 'reality'. Vertov draws attention to the processes by which a film is made. It might look real but 'realism' itself, he was saying, is partly a contrivance. The documentary film-maker Dai Vaughan, called THE MAN WITH A MOVIE CAMERA 'a study in film truth', and it is a fair description.

A different kind of truth was attempted by King Vidor in THE CROWD (1928). He had had a great success with THE BIG PARADE, which had essentially been structured around one ordinary man's observations of the First World War. He now had the idea of making a film that was what Vidor called, 'the saga of an average man and his day-to-day battle with the living of an ordinary life'. Focusing on a hero who is born in 1900, the dawn of a new age, Vidor charted the progress and hardships of a character who was basically just one of the crowd. 'I envisaged him as a sort of nondescript', said Vidor, 'but not a negative individual, the sort of fellow you could like and with whom you'd be sympathetic, but not too aggressive, not too active'. To adhere to his realist objective, Vidor deliberately chose a cast of relative unknowns: James Murray as the hero, Eleanor Boardman as the woman he marries. As far as possible he wanted to avoid an artificial plot structure, so the story concentrates on the familiar life pattern of the ordinary man: marriage and parenthood, employment and occasional unemployment, the periods of happiness (a day out at Coney Island) alternating with spells of tragedy (the death of his daughter, his lapse into alcoholism). Although the film affected a realistic style, it had passages of astonishing virtuos-ity (one camera movement tilts up a skyscraper until it finally isolates its hero in an impersonal, densely populated office), and remarkably perceptive performances. Tragically, the career of James Murray was to parallel that of the character he played: a man of enormous promise unable to capitalize on his ability, and descending into a suicidal alcoholism. Of all Vidor's films, THE CROWD is one that has stood the test of time. It gave an extremely incisive picture of American society immediately before the Wall Street crash, and offered a compassionate and complex view of the American Dream, as seen by a hero for whom it must remain an unattainable illusion.

THE CROWD demonstrated that film had come of age. It showed that the cinema was not simply a dream factory but could reflect ordinary lives. It also revealed that the camera was not simply a mechanical eye, but was a subtle and creative instrument that could heighten an audience's insight into other people's lives – and their own. Even so radical and innovative a film-maker as Jean-Luc Godard in the 1960s had to concede that Vidor was unsurpassed in his creation of the definitive film of the Common Man. When asked by financiers to make films 'for the people', Godard replied: 'The Crowd has already been made – why remake it?'

LEFT: Trying to silence the city's roar as his child lies dying: James Murray in *The Crowd*.

RIGHT: James Murray (left) and Eleanor Boardman (right) watch in helpless horror as their daughter is run over. From *The Crowd*.

ABOVE: *Quo Vadis*

CHAPTER EIGHT

The Greatest Show on Earth

'The cinema must give the spectators fantastic visions, lyric catastrophes, marvels born of the most sturdy imagination. As in the epic poems, it must bring back the marvelous, the super-marvelous, of today and tomorrow.' (Gabriele D'Annunzio)

The cinema had found that it could surpass the theater and other art forms in realism. Now, thought D'Annunzio, was the time for the cinema to surpass all other art forms in spectacle as well.

D'Annunzio was, so to speak, writing from first-hand experience. He had just been involved in writing the titles of one of the great epics of Italian silent cinema, CABIRIA (1914), directed by Giovanni Pastrone. Set during the time of the Punic Wars, CABIRIA recounted the story of the love-affair between a Sicilian slave girl, Cabiria, and a Roman. D'Annunzio's hand can be suspected in some of the more poetic of the film's titles: for example, 'He is like a wind, bringing the scent of dust and lions'. But audiences did not flock to CABIRIA for the poetry. What they relished most were the demonstrations of strength by the muscle man 'Maciste', who was the Steve Reeves of the Italian silent cinema; and the grand set-pieces, which included such diversions as Hannibal's crossing of the Alps, the spectacular eruption of Mount Etna, and the sacrifice of children in the Temple of Moloch at Carthage.

CABIRIA was not the first of its kind. It was preceded by Enrico Guazzoni's QUO VADIS? in 1912, which, while telling its main story of the love of a Roman soldier for a Christian girl, recreated on a colossal scale the glory, grandeur and brutality that was Rome. It was to be remade in 1924 and then again, amid much fanfare, by MGM in 1950, in full color and sound but otherwise with rather inferior grandeur. The early Italian epics established a pattern of conventions and situations which were to be repeated many times over the years in both the silent and sound era. The orgy, the big battle, the ceremonial entrance with the cheering crowds, the odd miracle, a natural disaster or two – all these were to become staple ingredients of the genre. So too were the character stereotypes of the muscular heroes and the mousy heroines. The main themes were either the moral development of an important man or national glory, but there was always to be a feeling of destiny and importance, of history about to be made.

QUO VADIS? was an immensely popular film of early cinema. When it opened in London it was

LEFT: Early Italian spectacle: *Cabiri*.

RIGHT: Stirring action in the epic, *Messalina*, made by *Quo Vadis* director, Enrico Guazzoni in 1923.

screened at the Royal Albert Hall to audiences of 20,000 people at a time. The economics of this were not lost on producers and directors, who began to sense that they must think bigger in every way and also recognized that the future of the cinema lay in feature-length films. One should not forget the artistic fallout either. D W Griffith was immensely impressed by this Italian grandeur, for it corresponded to his own grand designs for the cinema. Films like QUO VADIS? and CABIRIA lit the spark that was to lead Griffith towards making THE BIRTH OF A NATION and INTOLERANCE.

INTOLERANCE is still best remembered as the film that built Babylon rather than the movie that strove for universal brotherhood. Griffith released the Babylon section of the film, THE FALL OF BABYLON as a separate feature in 1919. All the deleted material was restored, and a new happy ending was tacked on, as hero (Elmer Clifton) and heroine (Constance Talmadge) found exile and happiness in distant Nineveh. The film historian William K Everson found this rather remarkable as Nineveh 'in actuality had been destroyed some two hundred years earlier'. Such

anachronisms were to become one of the most visible characteristics of the epic film in later years, as was concisely expressed in an anonymous poem that had wide circulations in film circles:

Cecil B De Mille,
Much against his will,
Was persuaded to keep Moses
Out of the Wars of the Roses.

INTOLERANCE had not originally been planned as an epic and indeed was one only intermittently in its final form. THE BIRTH OF A NATION might be regarded as more consistently epic in scheme, since it was centrally about national glory and a period that represented a crucial turning point in American history. Griffith was the first to see that, of all the pre-existing film forms in the American cinema, the one that lent itself to epic expansion most readily was the Western. Previously the Western had been regarded as a rather simple, low form, which was capable only of handling the theme of good versus evil in the most rudimentary terms (white shirt = hero, black shirt = villain etc). THE BIRTH OF A NATION hinted at a much larger theme for the Western: nothing less

ABOVE; The way west: *The Covered Wagon*.

RIGHT: Building the railroad: John Ford's *The Iron Horse*, starring George O'Brien (center).

LEFT: John Ford (right) squats in a camera pit to film a locomotive passing overhead in *The Iron Horse*. On the left, cameraman George Schneiderman; in the center, assistant cameraman Burnett Guffey.

than the creation of modern America, its heroic heritage, the winning of the West, and the bringing of civilization into the wilderness.

THE BIRTH OF A NATION is more commonly regarded as a historical epic than a Western. The first big epic Western was THE COVERED WAGON (1923), directed by James Cruze and edited by Dorothy Arzner (who was to become the first major woman director in Hollywood of the sound era). The cameraman Karl Brown, who had previously been an assistant to Griffith, was later to recall that Cruze had accepted the directing job with considerable lack of enthusiasm, for his opinion of Westerns at that time was similar to that of the writer Ben Hecht: 'movies about horses for horses'. What seemed to change his mind, remarkably enough, was a viewing of Robert Flaherty's NANOOK OF THE NORTH, which gave Cruze a new slant on the way to handle the material. As the film evolved Cruze found himself approaching THE COVERED WAGON less from the point of a view of a story than as a slice of history, a documentary reconstruction of the original trek. Like Flaherty, Cruze shifted the film's focus away from the individual towards the group and towards the event itself, which began to assume epic proportions as an important moment in the country's history. The film was an enormous success.

It was followed by an even more significant Western on a similar scale, THE IRON HORSE (1924), the first film to bring its young director John Ford to major critical attention. The epic event of this film was the building of the first American transcontinental railroad. To set a suitably grand tone one of Ford's great heroes of history, Abraham Lincoln appeared as a character in the first scene, expounding the theme of the nation 'pushing forward the inevitable path to the West'. It had many of the same ingredients as THE COVERED WAGON – a river crossing, a fight with Indians, a love story – but it had a more exciting narrative, structured around a hero's search for his father's murderer. One critic of the time called it 'an American Odyssey'. It was to be 15 years before Ford was to make STAGECOACH in 1939 and gradually come to dominate the genre more than any other director. ('My name's John Ford', he would later say at Directors' Guild meetings, 'I make Westerns'). But the traces of his future dominance were all there in THE IRON HORSE: the sense of communal solidarity and humor, the visual response to landscape, the vivid staging of action, but above all, the ability to turn this simple Western tale into a poetic celebration of nineteenth-century American progress. In this movie lay the seeds of what Ford became: the unsurpassed chronicler of pioneering America.

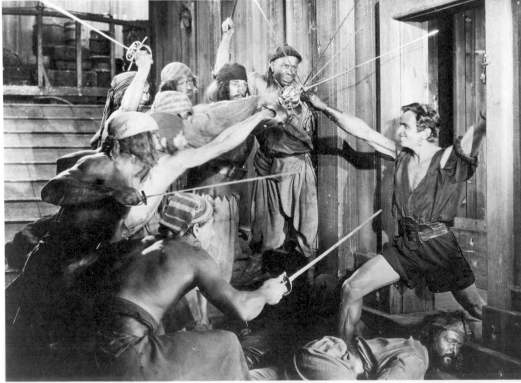

ABOVE: Typical acrobatics from Douglas Fairbanks as D'Artagnan in *The Three Musketeers*.

LEFT: Smiling swashbuckler: Fairbanks fences off the opposition in *The Black Pirate*.

RIGHT: Julianne Johnston (left), Anna May Wong (center) and Douglas Fairbanks (right) in *The Thief of Bagdad*.

If the Western was the form which more than any other turned the subject of America into an epic theme, the actor of the time who seemed to embody the spirit of America better than anyone was Douglas Fairbanks. It mattered little that the famous heroes he played on screen hailed from France, Nottingham and Bagdad. Fairbanks transfused them with the energy and optimism of America, and his acrobatic adventurism seemed the quintessence of New World confidence and virility. Fairbanks was seen to his best advantage in two of the most spectacular adventure-epics of the 1920s, ROBIN HOOD (1922) and THE THIEF OF BAGDAD (1924).

'I don't want to play a flat-footed Englishman walking through the woods', said Fairbanks, when the idea of making a film of Robin Hood was first mooted. But director Allan Dwan knew how to

tickle Fairbanks' interest in the theme. 'Just get some bows and arrows and a target,' he said. 'Doug is such a natural sportsman, that he'll become hooked on archery'. This was what happened. However, a second obstacle occurred when Fairbanks saw the set. The film had been designed by one of the great silent film art directors, Wilfred Buckland, and some of the sets, notably the enormous castle and a banqueting hall that stretched for over 450 feet, were bigger than the Babylon sets for INTOLERANCE. 'I can't compete with that,' Fairbanks said, but once Dwan had demonstrated how he might cut quite a dash by hanging from the drapes and vaulting round the imposing architecture, Fairbanks was convinced. It turned out to be one of Fairbanks's biggest successes, full of daring and the kind of humorous bravado that was his forte, beautifully photographed,

and with a specially commissioned score by Victor Schertzinger. A thoughtful note about the impermanence of the kind of restless spirit which Fairbanks epitomized was seen in the opening title, a quotation from Charles Kingsley's poem 'Old and New':

So fleet the works of men,
Back to their earth again,
Ancient and holy things
Fade like a dream.

Fairbanks' fame was to fade rapidly in the sound era as the years took their toll of his athleticism.

Fairbanks' other great success of the 1920s was THE THIEF OF BAGDAD (1924), directed by Raoul Walsh and in a somewhat different style from ROBIN HOOD. Fairbanks had been greatly impressed by some of the German fantasy films he had seen, particularly by Fritz Lang's DESTINY (1921), a tale of love and death that shifted locales between ancient China, seventeenth-century Venice and old Bagdad, and had some striking special effects. The aim of THE THIEF OF BAGDAD was to create a total fantasy world, with painted trees, architecture made to seem out of all proportion to its setting, all augmented by a larger-than-life hero who bounced through the action with seemingly supernatural leaps (actually aided by trampolines concealed out of sight of the camera). The sets were designed by William Cameron Menzies, who was to become famous for his art direction on such 1930s classics as THINGS TO COME (1936) and GONE WITH THE WIND (1939), and the cos-

tumes were the work of Mitchell Leisen, who was soon to become one of Hollywood's most successful directors of sophisticated romantic comedy/dramas, most notably MIDNIGHT (1939). Everything built towards a rousing and spectacular finale in which the palace was besieged and the thief and princess made their escape on a magic carpet – one of early Hollywood's most impressive special effects that dazzled audiences.

One director who above all others was to be associated in the public mind with the film epic was Cecil B De Mille. It was an association that began during the silent period, although, in fact, De Mille made a wide variety of films in the early part of his career that suggested that his range was greater than it later became. Many film historians believe that the epic was his downfall as a film artist but it was undoubtedly the making of him as a popular entertainer. He was to become known as 'God's publicity agent' and the 'greatest showman on earth'.

In his early films, such as THE CHEAT (1915), in which a spendthrift heroine (Fanny Ward) is compelled to sell herself to a Japanese financier (Sessue Hayakawa) to replace money for the Red Cross that she has gambled away, De Mille had been praised for his social and psychological realism, which put him not far below Griffith in esteem. Later in films like OLD WIVES FOR NEW (1918), DON'T CHANGE YOUR HUSBAND (1919) and WHY CHANGE YOUR WIFE? (1920), he was to become renowned for saucy and glossy

RIGHT: Cecil B De Mille in 1914, directing *The Call of the North.*

LEFT: Film on a grand scale: *The Thief of Bagdad.*

ABOVE; Degenerate Rome, as imagined in the famous flashback of Cecil B De Mille's *Manslaughter*.

LEFT: *Male and Female*: Swanson in Babylon.

RIGHT: A sleeping Gloria Swanson is approached by a real lion in *Male and Female*. 'Every hair on my head was standing on end, recalled Swanson. 'Every cell in my body quivered when the animal roared.'

romantic dramas, often starring Gloria Swanson, which flirted with the exciting prospect of extra-marital affairs even as they extolled the virtues of marriage. Once, when asked why so many of his films were about adultery, the Italian director, Vittorio de Sica had replied: 'But if you take adultery out of the lives of the bourgeoisie, what have they left?' In a sense many of De Mille's films were about that, full of the ambience and aspirations of suburbia – all luxurious bedrooms and bathrooms – but with characters of an interesting emotional brittleness, rather like figures out of Scott Fitzgerald, and craving excitement. In general though, De Mille clearly endorsed rather than criticized this life style. 'I believe that my films have had an obvious effect on American life', he said in 1926. 'I have brought a certain sense of beauty and luxury into everyday existence, all jokes about ornate bathrooms and deluxe boudoirs aside. I have done my bit towards lifting the level of daily life'. He was about to do his bit towards lifting the moral tone of the screen as well.

One curiosity of his films until the mid-1920s was his tendency to include in his modern stories a flash-back sequence to earlier times. Sometimes, as when the characters imagine they are in Babylon in MALE AND FEMALE (1919) it seemed mainly an excuse to give Gloria Swanson a change of wardrobe. In ADAM'S RIB (1923), a brief vision of prehistoric days seemed thematically relevant. Most famously, in MANSLAUGHTER (1922), when an heiress's reckless driving leads to the death of a traffic policeman, De Mille visually likened her callous Jazz Age behavior to degenerate Romans in the days immediately before the fall of the Empire, which gave him the cue to slip in an elaborate orgy. This was all part of De Mille's gift: to give you the sermon against sin while also allowing an audience vicariously to enjoy its excesses. Such inclusions, however, were a pointer to the direction of De Mille's future career.

In 1923 in association with the *Los Angeles Times*, De Mille organized a contest for the public to choose the subject for his next film. It was a good publicity stunt, of course, but it also reflected De Mille's interest in public taste which he would gauge more

successfully than any American film maker prior to Steven Spielberg. On studying the entries De Mille was struck by the number of suggestions for films on a Biblical theme. This was the time when the public outrage caused by the Hollywood scandals of 1921 and 1922 was still in the air, and the film capital was under considerable pressure to clean up its act. The

ABOVE: A tense moment from the Biblical prologue of Cecil B De Mille's *The Ten Commandments*.

RIGHT: The Crucifixion in *The King of Kings*.

son of an Episcopalian minister and a man of rigidly conservative views, De Mille might well have sensed that this was a propitious time to make a film with a Biblical message after his own heart. The theme was inspired by the winning entry in the contest which was sent in by a manufacturer of lubricating oil in Michigan and which simply stated as its subject: 'you cannot break the Ten Commandments – they will break you'.

Because of the immense popularity of his remake of THE TEN COMMANDMENTS in 1956, which concentrated exclusively on the Biblical story, it is sometimes forgotten that his 1923 version was mainly a modern story with a Biblical prologue. The modern story contrasted the careers of two brothers, one of whom obeyed the Commandments and one of whom flouted them. The philandering materialist only realizes the error of his ways when a building he has constructed using cheap materials collapses and kills his mother, but by then repentance is too late. Audiences of the time were most taken with the prologue, dealing with the flight of the Israelites from Egypt, which was enhanced by some technical innovations. The parting of the Red Sea was filmed in an early two-color technique, and made a huge impact.

De Mille's next major extravaganza was THE KING OF KINGS (1927), in which H B Warner played Christ. It was a controversial subject and the cast was instructed, indeed contracted, to be on its best behavior. De Mille's crafty dramatic sense was particularly evident at the film's opening: 'I decided to jolt the audience out of their preconceptions with an opening scene that none of them would be expecting: a lavish party in the luxurious home of a woman of Magdala, and that beautiful courtesan surrounded by the leering sensual faces of her admirers who taunt her because one of their number, young Judas, has evidently found the company of some wandering carpenter more interesting. . .' It is a good example of De Mille's thinking and his cunning blend of didacticism and depravity. Much as he loved his sermonizing soap-box, he also understood that the supreme thing in spectacle was sensuality and action: chases, parades, crashes, catastrophes. He was to remain unrivaled in this field of film-making until his death in 1959.

Something of De Mille's flair was evident in another classic epic of the period, BEN-HUR (1926) adapted from General Lew Wallace's best-selling novel and directed by Fred Niblo. Ramon Novarro played the title role and Francis X Bushman was cast

as the Roman, Messala, formerly Ben-Hur's closest friend who becomes his implacable enemy (a part that was played in the original stage production by William S Hart, before his days as a Western star). The human drama, however, took second place to the excitement of the sea battle and particularly to the frenzy of the chariot race. Like THE TEN COMMANDMENTS, BEN-HUR had its share of fatalities during the making, of both extras and horses. The work of the stuntmen in those days was by no means as professional as it is today, and film making on an epic scale was a dangerous as well as costly operation.

For one or two exceptional obsessives, however, the cinema was worth such danger. 'For me, the cinema is not just pictures. It is something great, mysterious and sublime, for which one should not spare any effort and for which one should not fail to risk one's life if the need arise'. So said the French director, Abel Gance, who had achieved an estimable reputation with such early masterpieces as J'ACCUSE (1919), and now sought to make his crowning achievement, NAPOLEON (1926). When told by a nurse that 42 extras had been injured during the filming of the taking of Toulon harbor, Gance replied: 'That's a good sign; the boys are putting their heart into it'. When his leading actor Albert Dieudonné attempted to leap from his horse into a boat and instead fell into the water, Dieudonné, who could not swim, was so immersed in the role that he cried out: 'Save Bonaparte! Save Bonaparte!'

The film concentrated on Napoleon's early life,

and lasted over five hours. Gance's conception of Napoleon was of a man who was to some degree a victim of destiny, 'dragged towards war by a chain of circumstances he was unable to escape'. The real star of the film, though, was Gance, who freed the camera in a way the cinema had rarely seen. He tied it to a running horse to film a hectic chase. On another occasion he mounted it on a giant pendu-lum, crosscutting between Napoleon in a stormy sea and the Paris Convention locked in argument, and swinging the camera back and forth. It was as if the camera itself were being rocked by the force of the political storms and waves of revolution that were sweeping France. The film deployed color, super-imposition, slow motion, split screen, sometimes alluded to great art in its screen compositions (like the murder of Marat, which was posed as in David's famous painting) and having also a specially com-missioned score by Arthur Honegger. Gance's most awesome innovation was the use of Polyvision, a triple screen process that anticipated Cinemascope and Cinerama by 30 years. Polyvision could show simultaneously what ordinary cinema could only show in succession. 'Think of the departure of the

LEFT: Messala (Francis X Bushman, left) taunts Ben-Hur (Ramon Novarro, center) during the pulsating chariot race of *Ben-Hur*.

BELOW: The sea battle in *Ben-Hur*, so authentically staged that it caused serious panic among the extras.

army of Italy for the Po Valley in NAPOLEON', said Jean-Luc Godard. 'On the center screen, a battalion on the march; on the side screens, Bonaparte galloping along a road. The effect is striking. After a few minutes we feel we have traveled all the thousands of kilometers of that prodigious Italian campaign'. For Gance, Polyvision was essentially a poetic device. The central screen carried the story, the theme, but the side screen carried the mental, the emotional, the metaphorical dimensions of the theme. On the central screen, the story, he said, was prose; the side screen, the wings, were poetry.

The premiere at the Paris Opera House in 1927 was a triumph. 'The day of the Image has arrived', cried Gance, triumphantly. Tragically, he was wrong. The day of Sound was just about to arrive in the cinema and the day of the Image correspondingly diminished, with Polyvision becoming almost instantly obsolete. It was to be over 50 years before NAPOLEON was able to be reconstructed in something approximating its original form (sadly, Gance had destroyed most of his original Polyvision scenes in a fit of despair, and only the Italian campaign which concludes the film still remains in that form). It is some testimony to the epic audacity and endurance of the silent cinema that a film made in 1926, when shown in the form intended, could become one of the major cinematic events of the 1980s. 'From now on', said the head of the British Film Institute, Anthony Smith, after the triumphant showing of the restored version of the film in London, 'there will be two kinds of people in the world: those who have, or have not, seen NAPOLEON'.

ABOVE: The battle of Toulon in *Napoleon*.

RIGHT: Napoleon (Albert Dieudonné) and Josephine (Gina Manès).

LEFT: Preparing to film the snowball fight in *Napoleon*. Gance's camera mobility was phenomenal and the overall effect was received with a standing ovation at the gala premiere.

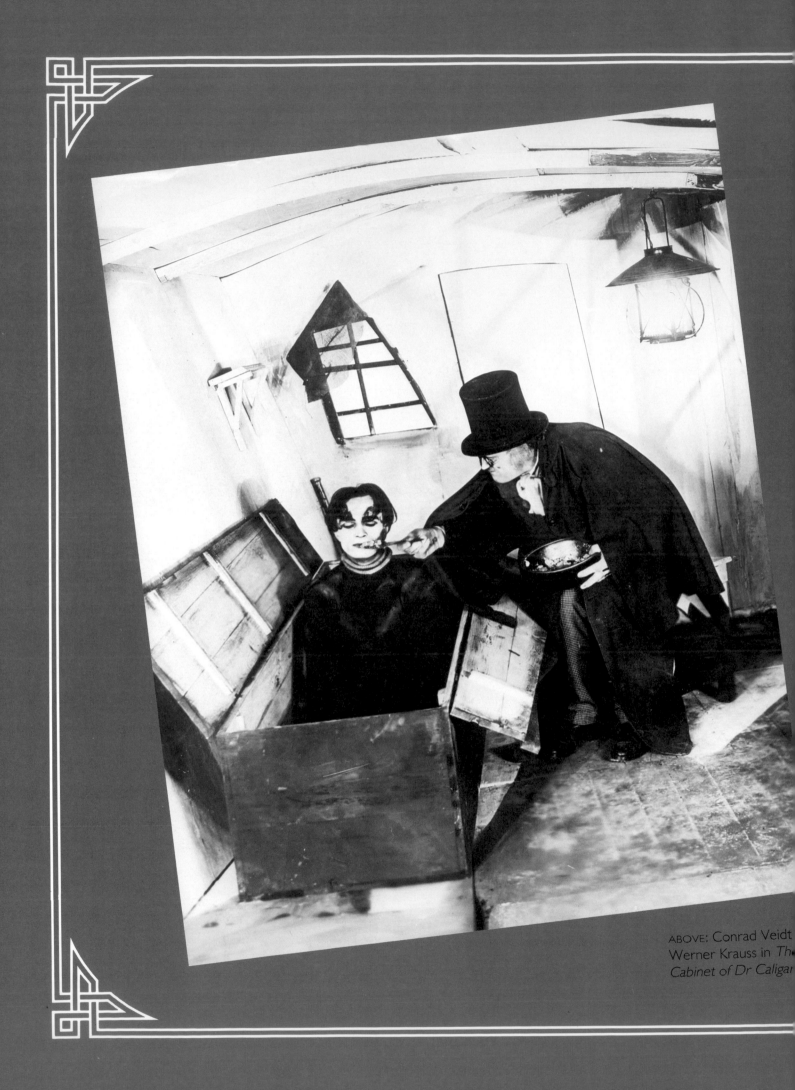

CHAPTER NINE
European Masters

'If you think this picture's no good, I'll put on a
beard and say it was made in Germany: then
you'll call it art'. (Title in *Will Rogers*' comedy,
THE ROPIN' FOOL)

From its early days, Hollywood has traditionally been associated with commerce and escapism, and European cinema with seriousness and art. It has never been that simple: some remarkable artists have operated successfully within the American system, and arty European cinema has sometimes tended towards the pretentious and the cumbersome. Yet the profit motive was invariably paramount in Hollywood's eyes; the rapid development of the star system seemed to emphasize glamour more than profundity; and even clearly prodigious talents like John Ford would insist modestly and even grumpily, that film direction was less an artistic endeavor anyway than simply 'a job of work'.

Hollywood's unjustified sense of inferiority might have been influenced by Europe's early condescending attitude towards cinema in some circles. In Germany in 1912, stage actors were expressly forbidden to appear on screen and, as we have seen, the great theatrical stars like Bernhardt and Forbes-Robertson made films not out of any interest in the medium but as a means of preserving their dramatic immortality. With the exception of Scandinavia, European cinema was almost comprehensively inferior to America until 1920, when, for a variety of reasons shortly to be examined, there was a sudden explosion of creative talent and experimentation in film throughout Europe. Typically, Hollywood's answer to this threat of competing excellence was an attempt to buy it off. During the 1920s it poached an enormous number of actors, actresses and directors from Europe, some of whom were to go from strength to strength, like Greta Garbo or Ernst Lubitsch, and others who were to find the American film factory distinctly uncongenial, like Emil Jannings, and Pola Negri, and the Swedish directors Victor Sjöstrom and Mauritz Stiller.

Sjöstrom and Stiller dominated Swedish cinema in the early years of the century and, for many, they are the greatest of early European film-makers. Indeed, Sjöstrom has sometimes been compared favorably with Griffith. He might not have had Griffith's filmic flair, but he avoided the latter's melodramatic excesses, and his films had a social concern and moral severity that highlighted the cinema's unsuspected powers of both propaganda and psychology. The impact of his denunciation of social conditions in Sweden in INGEBORG HOLM (1913) has already been discussed, yet his mastery was equally apparent in the supernatural world of THE PHANTOM CARRIAGE (1920), whose complicated time structure, with flashbacks within flashbacks, seemed to anticipate the work of Alain Resnais by 40 years. Perhaps, his greatest achievement was TERJE VIGEN (1916), a tragic saga based on a poem by Henrik Ibsen about a fisherman (played by Sjöstrom) separ-

ated from his wife and child during the Napoleonic Wars when he is arrested for attempting to break through the English blockade. Sjöstrom's work seemed to embody all the best characteristics of Swedish cinema at this time: a religious seriousness of purpose, an eloquent use of landscape to enhance the drama, an awareness of and sensitivity to social problems, and a naturalistic and restrained style of screen acting. When Swedish cinema went into something of a decline in the early 1920s, Sjöstrom went to Hollywood to study American methods of production, was signed up as a director by MGM, and changed his name to Victor Seastrom.

His Hollywood period was distinguished by two particularly outstanding films with Lillian Gish. His film version of Nathanial Hawthorne's classic Puritan novel, THE SCARLET LETTER (1926), with Lillian Gish as the adulteress Hester Prynne, was particularly notable for its visual quality, the scenes in the wood and on the scaffold fully matching the pictorial brilliance of the novel. Even more remarkable was THE WIND (1928), the story of a Virginian girl (Lillian Gish) forced into a marriage with a cowboy she does not love and then sexually menaced by a

LEFT: The European star, Pola Negri, admired for her passionate, earthy screen personality.

ABOVE: Lillian Gish in *The Wind*, directed by the Swedish master, Victor Sjöstrom (known as 'Seastrom' in Hollywood).

stranger. Seastrom built the tale into a study of frail femininity and turbulent nature, in which a desert storm comes to suggest overwhelming passions that might bury the characters. Not since BROKEN BLOSSOMS had Lillian Gish such an opportunity to exhibit the extreme emotional range of her acting. Although subsequently recognized as a classic, the film was suppressed at the time by MGM, according to Lillian Gish, because of an argument she had with the head of the studio, Louis B Mayer. 'He wanted to knock me off my pedestal, as he put it,' she said, 'and arrange a nice juicy scandal to pump up my career. Well, I didn't have any affairs. And I told him I just couldn't go along with it. So he ruined me. I had just finished THE WIND and he killed it.' Sjöstrom returned to Sweden shortly after this experience, and

spent most of the remainder of his career in acting roles. His most memorable, shortly before his death in 1960, was as the ageing professor reevaluating his life in Ingmar Bergman's WILD STRAWBERRIES (1957). It was the apotheosis of his acting career, and the association could not have been more appropriate, for his legacy was to live on most powerfully in the films of Bergman.

Although Sjöstrom never considered him so, for he had too much respect for his colleague's ability, his great rival at this time in Swedish film was the director Mauritz Stiller. Stiller's style was different from Sjöstrom's, less soberly serious, more flashy and technically adventurous, with a recurrent fascination with strong heroines. His most famous film was GOSTA BERLINGS SAGA (1924) – also known as THE ATONEMENT OF GOSTA BERLING – an episodic tale of love and hate, focusing particularly on a defrocked pastor, Gosta Berling, and his redemptive love for an Italian girl, Elizabeth, played by Stiller's discovery, Greta Garbo. When, like Sjöstrom, he was also signed up by MGM, he took Garbo with him to Hollywood, only to be dismayed to find that he was not expected to direct Garbo's pictures. In fact,

Stiller was to make only one significant film in America, for Paramount, HOTEL IMPERIAL (1926), starring Pola Negri, before returning to Sweden. He died in a Swedish hospital in 1928, with a photograph of Garbo clutched in his hand.

Although Swedish film particularly caught the eye during the silent period, Scandinavian cinema was also honorably represented by the Danes. Benjamin Christensen's NIGHT OF REVENGE (1915) was one of the European cinema's most extraordinary silent films, deploying advanced camera work and conjuring up a nightmarish atmosphere for its tale of a released prisoner who searches for his child. The Danish HAMLET (1920) put forward a remarkable thesis for the character's complexities and delays: he was a woman, the part being played by Asta Nielsen. Other English literary classics to receive original treatment were the works of Charles Dickens, whose novels were adapted – or more accurately, distilled – for the screen by A W Sandberg: GREAT EXPECTATIONS in 1921, DAVID COPPERFIELD in 1922, and LITTLE DORRITT in 1924. Undoubtedly the most famous and acclaimed Danish film of the silent era, though, was Carl Dreyer's THE PASSION OF JOAN OF ARC (1928), an austere account of the last 24 hours in Joan of Arc's life, with a remarkable performance in the title role by the celebrated actress of the Paris stage, Falconetti. It was to be her only screen performance (understandably she found the experience very harrowing), but it was of a quality, unlike many screen performances of her theatrical contemporaries, that assured her of a place in film history.

If Swedish cinema appeared to be the most interesting of the European cinemas during the years of the First World War, one factor was undoubtedly the historical one of its neutrality during the war: it was not subject to the same pressures and conditions of other European countries. However, the national cinema which made the biggest international impact in the immediate postwar years was undoubtedly the German cinema. The reasons for this development are too complex and various to summarize adequately. It might have been a desire to restore German culture in the eyes of the world, after the vilification of the Germans during the war. It might have been a desire to make up for lost cinematic ground – unlike the situation in France

RIGHT: Conrad Veidt (left) as Ivan the Terrible, foreseeing his death in his giant hourglass. One of the stories in *Waxworks*.

LEFT: Conrad Veidt carries off Lil Dagover in *The Cabinet of Dr Caligari*. The Expressionist decor emphasizes the sinister atmosphere.

and Italy, for example, there seemed to be little creative interest in film in Germany before and during the war. During the early 1920s, however, there was an explosion of artistic experimentation there as elsewhere, and it was inevitable that the newest of the art forms would be included in this. Moreover it was a period of harsh economic conditions and social upheaval, and the movie camera seemed an invaluable instrument to reflect this. Stirrings of a new quality in German film were first signaled by the early films of Ernst Lubitsch, such as CARMEN (1918), with Pola Negri, MADAME DUBARRY (1919) and THE OYSTER PRINCESS (1919). These were films which demonstrated a skill at historical drama but also a subtle satirical tone which became known, particularly after his later American classics such as NINOTCHKA (1939) and TO BE OR NOT TO BE (1942), as the 'Lubitsch touch'. But if there was one German film which particularly captured attention and seemed to encapsulate the new Germanic style, that film was THE CABINET OF DR CALIGARI (1919), directed by Robert Wiene.

Ostensibly, CALIGARI was a murder mystery, about a series of killings that seemed to be traceable to a fairground entertainer, Caligari (Werner Krauss), and his assistant, the somnabulist Cesare (Conrad Veidt). The twist in the tale is that the story is being narrated by a lunatic in an asylum, whose director is none other than Caligari himself. But is the story real or fantasy, a symptom of the narrator's madness or the cause of it? More remarkable than the story was

the visual style, particularly the use of shadow, harsh lighting and deliberately unreal, painted sets to reflect a disordered and distorted world, which in turn reflected the narrator's state of mind. 'Films must be drawings brought to life', said one of the designers, Hermann Warm, and in this film, decor was its most expressive element. Some deplored its artificiality, and even the writers were unhappy about the director's surprise ending, feeling that it undermined the critique of mad authority that they wanted to express. Yet others were very excited by it, the writer Virginia Woolf for example, admiring its ability to visualize inner thought and, as it were, to show the shape of fear. What it did more than anything was to herald the shape of a substantial, memorable part of German film for the next five years.

After CALIGARI, there was a host of films that had a similarly macabre, supernatural air, that seemed inspired by Gothic horror and fascinated by disturbed psychology. Arthur Robison's WARNING SHADOWS (1923) concerned a cuckolded husband who invited a showman to his house; the showman then hypnotizes his guests into revealing their secret desires. In Paul Leni's WAXWORKS (1924), a poet at a fairground waxworks museum wrote stories about some of the exhibits – Ivan the Terrible, Jack the Ripper. The latter character was to be the nemesis of the amoral heroine (Louise Brooks) of G W Pabst's PANDORA'S BOX (1929). On a more realistic level, E A Dupont's VARIETY (1925) was a study of jealousy and

revenge simmering backstage in a music hall, though here again the variety setting seemed to mock and heighten the emotional drama in a very expressive way, and its tone of Germanic gloom was certainly par for the course.

It has often been said that this period of German film was dominated more by its writers, actors, designers and cameramen than its directors, but nevertheless, two major directors did emerge from this Expressionist explosion. One was F W Murnau, who came to prominence with NOSFERATU (1922), the screen's first version of the Dracula story. Part of its terror came, unusually, from its being shot on location and having a basic realism, as if the evil (terrifyingly embodied by Max Schreck) unleashed on a complacent community, and the terrible sacrifice it would exact before its infection could be checked, had a particular relevance to contemporary Germany. Like CALIGARI, the film came to be seen, perhaps simplistically, as a prophecy of Nazism. Perhaps for this reason, but certainly also for its psychological complexity and its sinister imagery (the phantom ship, the monster's looming shadow), the modern German director, Werner Herzog was to acclaim this 'symphony of terror' as

'the most important film ever made in Germany', and remade it in 1979.

Murnau followed NOSFERATU with a film that was even more widely admired, THE LAST LAUGH (1924). Emil Jannings starred as the hotel commissionaire reduced to the position of lavatory attendant, the loss of status and uniform precipitating physical and mental degeneration conveyed through feverish images of the man's drunken fantasies. The film was praised for the fact that it had no titles; for its hallucinatory images of the city; for Jannings's extraordinary performance; and even for the symbolism of the hotel's revolving door, a wheel of fortune that would eventually see the hero rescued from his depths of degradation and despondency. On the strength of this film Murnau was invited to Hollywood, and he immediately made one of the acknowledged masterpieces of American silent film, SUNRISE (1927), a country versus city drama, enhanced by lyrical photography and remarkable performances. His last film, TABU (1931) involved him in an unhappy collaboration with Robert Flaherty; tragically, a week before the film's premiere, Murnau was killed in a car crash. He was only forty-two.

Roughly at the time of Murnau's death, the other

FAR LEFT: Louise Brooks as Lulu, with Franz Lederer on her lap, in *Pandora's Box*.

ABOVE LEFT: The traveling players: *Variety*.

BOTTOM LEFT: 'The stifling shadow of the vampire vanished with the morning sun'. Max Schreck in *Nosferatu*.

RIGHT: Tormented dreams in *The Last Lught*.

great director of the German silent cinema, Fritz Lang, was also preparing to leave Germany for Hollywood, but for very different reasons: he had been offered the job of the head of the German film industry by the Third Reich, and he wanted no part of it. Lang's reputation in the 1920s had been forged by his imaginative and chilling portrait of a superman master-criminal in DR MABUSE THE GAMBLER (1922), and his Wagnerian epic on the Siegfried legend, DIE NIBELUNGEN (1924). But his most spectacular achievement was METROPOLIS (1926), a futuristic vision of the modern city that took nearly a year to shoot, involved over 30,000 extras and was the most expensive German film made up to that time. Its final advocacy of a humanistic harmony between Capital and Labor even at the time seemed a trifle naive, but the message was quite overwhelmed by the visuals: the City as Prison; the City as Moloch, devouring its children; a mad scientist Rotwang, who, philosophically and even visually, seemed a strong anticipation of Dr Strangelove. It was Hitler's favorite film, which no doubt influenced his offer to Lang of the foremost film post in the land: he saw the ending as showing that responsible rule is a matter of reconciling heart with head. But another interpretation of METROPOLIS – the portrait of a wicked

LEFT: George O'Brien and Margaret Livingstone in F W Murnau's *Sunrise*.

BOTTOM LEFT: Rudolph Klein-Rogge (second from left) as the master-criminal Dr Mabuse in Fritz Lang's *Dr Mabuse – the Gambler* (1922).

RIGHT: The death of Siegfried: Part One of Lang's *Die Nibelungen*.

BELOW: The mad scientist Rotwang (Rudolph Klein-Rogge) constructs a false Maria (Brigitte Helm) to incite and demoralize the workers in *Metropolis*.

ABOVE: The brutal architecture of *Metropolis*.

LEFT: Sergei Eisenstein with his eye to the camera.

RIGHT: Eisenstein lines up a shot for his first feature, *Strike*. Operating the camera is his regular cameraman, Eduard Tisse.

city with madmen in control – might equally explain Lang's refusal of the offer and his flight to America. He was to be joined by fellow emigrées like Robert Siodmak and Billy Wilder who, along with other future exiles, Fred Zinnemann and the cameraman Eugene Schüfftan, all collaborated on one of the last major German films of its most creative and turbulent decade, PEOPLE ON SUNDAY (1929).

It was the aftermath of the First World War, and the social and artistic convulsions engendered by it, that had galvanized German cinema and shot it to world prominence. It was the aftermath of the Russian Revolution that catapulted the next major national cinema to the forefront of world attention: that of the Soviet Union. 'They were astonishing and wonderful days', recalled the director Sergei Yutkevitch of the post-revolutionary period, which was really to achieve its creative apex between 1924 and 1929. 'When we talk about the years when we began to work, people are always surprised by the birth dates of almost all the directors and important artists of those times. We were incredibly young. We were sixteen and seventeen years old when we started into our artistic lives. The explanation is quite simple: the revolution had made way for the young'. Small wonder that so many young artists gravitated towards the cinema which was not only the newest of the art forms, but had the largest audience and was therefore potentially the most influential. Moreover it had the endorsement of the Party leadership. 'For us', said Lenin, 'the cinema is the most important of the arts'.

Crucially cinema became part of the whole atmosphere of artistic ferment where the young were searching for new means of expression and rejecting tradition and convention. A young scientist, Vsevolod Pudovkin saw D W Griffith's INTOLERANCE and was so taken aback that he changed profession. He had been particularly impressed by Griffith's use of montage as an advanced form of story-telling, but he was even more intrigued when, in the experimental laboratory of his colleague Lev Kuleshov, Kuleshov seemed to demonstrate that the meaning of a shot could be changed according to the shot with which it was linked. Kuleshov showed an actor responding to a shot of a plate of soup, then a dead woman in a coffin, then a little girl with a toy, and the actor was praised for the way he displayed hunger, then grief, then happiness. Kuleshov then revealed that it was actually the same face: the meaning had been altered not by subtle gradations of performance but by juxtaposition of shots. Pudovkin was greatly influenced by this theory of 'linkage', as it was called, but also placed a great stress on acting and the performer. Many of his ideas were evident in his first feature, MOTHER (1926), based on a novel by Maxim Gorky,

and dealing with the situation of a family torn apart by a strike. His instinctive mastery of film technique was demonstrated by his manner of conveying the inner mood of the shattered and exhausted mother. 'Her exhaustion,' he explained, 'is underlined by photographing her from above so that it looks as if this exhaustion is driving her into the ground'.

Yet Kuleshov's and Pudovkin's theories of monteage were not universally acceptable. Sergei Eisenstein, who had trained to be an engineer, but whom the Revolution, in his words, 'had made into an artist', believed that montage should not be 'linkage': montage should be 'shock'. He coined a term for his method: cinema fist. Something of the power of his punch was felt in his first feature, STRIKE (1924), when he crosscut the sequence of the massacre of the strikers with shots of an animal being slaughtered in an abattoir. A linkage of ideas, certainly, to suggest the massacre as an act of political butchery. But it was more than that: it was also a desire to arouse an audience's sense of horror and outrage through this savage and shocking juxtaposition of events. His next film not only shocked: it was to become one of the enduring classics of the cinema.

The original idea behind BATTLESHIP POTEMKIN (1925) was of a film that would commemorate the twentieth anniversary of the first abortive Revolution in 1905. But as the film developed, Eisenstein decided to concentrate on just one incident during that time: the circumstances that surrounded the mutiny of the sailors on the battleship *Potemkin*. Eisenstein was working at white heat to finish the film on time, and perhaps, his most significant decision was, because of adverse weather conditions, to transfer the shooting of the film from Leningrad

to Odessa. As soon as he arrived at Odessa and saw those steps, he knew he had to use them in a big scene in the film. He could not know that he was creating one of the most powerful and widely imitated sequences in film history.

The Odessa steps sequence in POTEMKIN, which recorded the moment when Cossack soldiers opened fire on the civilian population, was an incomparable dramatization of collective panic, but interestingly, was also a very calculated demonstration of Eisenstein's theories of montage in action. The conflict of the scene was heightened by the calculated conflict of images: still shots followed by moving shots, upward movement followed by downward movement, the rigid pattern of marching boots followed by the chaotic pattern of mass panic. Individual detail underlined the horror. A student's face symbolized individual helplessness; a Cossack's slashing sword encapsulated the brutality of the military; an unforgettable close-up of an old woman, her glasses broken and blood streaming from one eye (an image so shocking, it was cut from some prints) proclaimed the film's rage and its rebuke of the soldiers' action. It was an astonishing achievement for a film that had no stars: its heroes were the common people. It terrified many authorities in the West, who thought the film had the power to make revolutionaries of us all. For years after, the screening of this film in the capitals of Europe could result in prosecution or even imprisonment.

Eisenstein was not really to emulate the power of POTEMKIN, though in OCTOBER (1928), he achieved a film that was at once epic and satirical. However his

ОКТЯБРЬ

RIGHT: V Nikandrov as Lenin in Eisenstein's *October*, a recreation of revolutionary events in Russia.

BELOW RIGHT: Maggoty meat: a cause for mutiny in *Battleship Potemkin*.

LEFT: Eisenstein's *Strike*, a film without individual heroes but with the masses as a collective hero against oppression.

development of intellectual montage was above the heads of many of his audience and the critics, and he was to run into criticisms of 'formalism' – an engagement with style at the expense of Socialist content – that were periodically to dog his career until his death in 1948, the same year as his mentor and inspiration, Griffith. In general the steam was running out of the more advanced, experimental, exciting phase of Soviet cinema. One of its last manifestations was Grigori Kozintsev's and Leonid Trauberg's NEW BABYLON (1929), about the Paris Commune of 1871 and adorned by a spiky score from one of the century's great composers of film (or any other) music, Dimitri Shostakovich.

There was another strand of adventurism in European cinema, and it came in the form of Surrealism, which was an avant-garde form of film, often obscure though playful, and often thumbing its nose at the values of modern bourgeois society. A playful example of surrealism was René Clair's ENTR'ACTE (1924), designed as an interlude for Erik Satie's score for the ballet *Relâche*, and generally coloring the surrealism with a slyness and slapstick that anticipated Clair's comic masterpieces such as AN ITALIAN STRAW HAT (1927). The Japanese film A PAGE OF MADNESS (1926), directed by Teinosuke Kinugasa (who was to make the famous GATE OF HELL in 1954) was rediscovered by the director in his garden shed in 1972 and revealed a catalog of complex visual devices

to illustrate the disturbed world of the asylum in which it was set. It stood on its head the previous received wisdom that Japanese silent film was technically cautious and conservative. Surrealism at its most impenetrable was illustrated by Germaine Dullac's THE SEASHELL AND THE CLERGYMAN (1928), a film so obscure that it was refused a certificate by the British Board of Film Censors for that reason alone. 'The film is so cryptic as to be almost meaningless,' said the censor. 'If there is a meaning, it is doubtless objectionable.'

There was no doubt about the intentional meaninglessness of Luis Buñuel's and Salvador Dali's UN CHIEN ANDALOU (1929), nor about its equally intended offensiveness. Buñuel, who had already revealed an original cast of mind by stating in an essay that he thought Buster Keaton a far better film actor than Emil Jannings, called the film a 'passionate, desperate appeal to murder'. He and Dali intended it as a succession of images to which no meaning could be put, though this did not stop people from interpreting it as, among other things, an evocation of the world of dreams, an oblique picture of the battle of the sexes, or an attack on the dead-weight of culture. Some of its images – an eye sliced by a razor, a hand crawling with ants – were genuinely upsetting and disturbing. Curiously though, a lot of the film's themes and images (madness, murder, shifting sexual identity, an obsession with eyes and sharp

LEFT: Pudovkin's *The End of St Petersburg*: a celebrated sequence crosscuts war footage with shots of speculators at the stock exchange.

ABOVE: Outrageous imagery in *Un Chien Andalou*. Making sexual advances to the girl (Simone Mareuil), the hero (Pierre Batcheff) finds himself jerked back (repressed?) by a variety of dead weights – priests, a piano, and dead mules.

RIGHT: Rumpus over a hat: René Clair's *An Italian Straw Hat*.

instruments) were all eventually to find their way into one of the mainstream cinema's biggest hits of 1960, Alfred Hitchcock's PSYCHO.

And what was the young Hitchcock up to at this time? He was finding his voice. Having made a Jack the Ripper-type thriller, THE LODGER in 1926, which was full of influences of the German cinema, he returned to the thriller form in 1929 in BLACKMAIL and made his first really characteristic film. It might also have been the first movie really to use the innovation of sound. Hitchcock had begun BLACKMAIL as a silent, but then introduced sound into key sequences. One became a classic of its kind: the heroine had knifed a seducer to death, and is having breakfast with her family the next morning. A neighbor enters and starts talking about the murder. After a while, the only word one can hear clearly is the word 'knife' which begins to stab at the heroine's conscience, pressing on it like a sensitive nerve. She reaches for the breadknife, at which point the neighbor suddenly says 'KNIFE!' very loudly and the knife flies from her hand. It was Hitchcock's way of suggesting the girl's inner tension, and how the crime is preying on her mind. It was a hopeful signal that showed sound could be used as creatively as a camera, for by 1929, the Golden Age of silent cinema was over.

BELOW: Daisy Jackson (left) and Ivor Novello in Alfred Hitchcock's first thriller, *The Lodger*.

RIGHT: Gordon Harker (left), Carl Brisson (center) and Harry Terry (right) in the opening fairground scene from Hitchcock's *The Ring*.

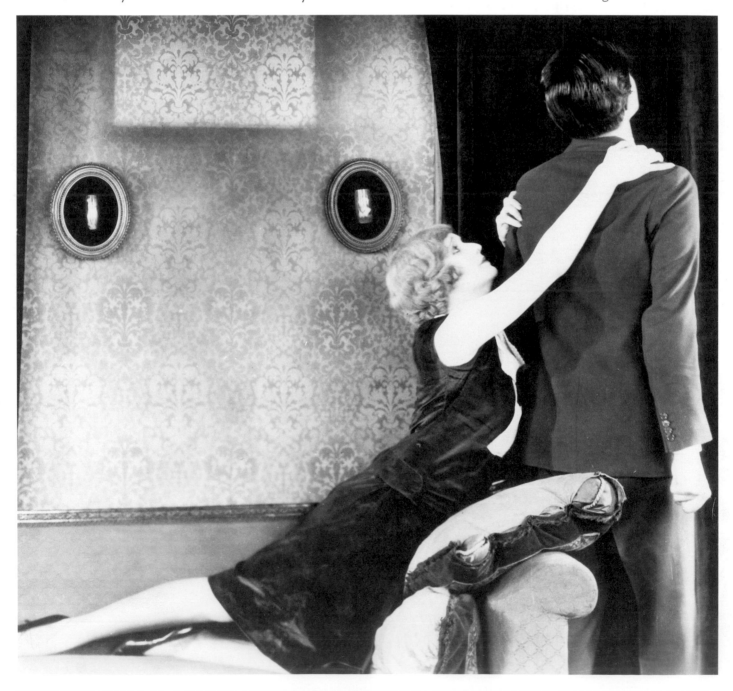

ABOVE: D W Griffith
directs his first sound

CHAPTER TEN
Silent Sunset

There is a story that Sam Goldwyn was dining in
a Hollywood restaurant with Billy Wilder when he
was accosted by a drunk demanding work. The
man became so obstreperous that Goldwyn, with
the aid of some of the restaurant staff, had to
escort him out of the building. 'Who was that?'
Wilder asked when Goldwyn resumed his seat.
'D W Griffith,' replied Goldwyn.

Griffith, Gance, John Gilbert: these are some of the names that immediately float to the surface when one is thinking of giants of the silents who became casualties of sound. Yet to blame the coming of sound for their decline would be an oversimplification. Griffith was in a creative decline some time before the arrival of the sound era. Gance was the kind of cinematic figure who, like Stroheim, Orson Welles and, in the modern age, Michael Cimino, would always have difficulty in accommodating his grandiose visions to the commercial requirements of the cinema: Polyvision might have been a remarkable idea but, commercially, it was simply the wrong innovation at the wrong time. John Gilbert's tragic demise as a screen romantic hero had less to do with his supposedly high pitched voice than with the fact that that kind of hero now seemed irredeemably dated in a harsher era. Also, like Lillian Gish, Buster Keaton and the talented director Marshall Neilan, Gilbert had made an enemy of MGM's Louis B Mayer, who was not a forgiving man. Mayer, more than the microphone, might have put the skids under the careers of some of the most gifted people of the silent era. The sound revolution had happened very quickly. Within two years of Al Jolson's declaration in THE JAZZ SINGER (1927) that 'you ain't heard nothing yet', the silent film was effectively dead and cinemas around the world were beginning to install new sound equipment. The movement towards the introduction of sound in cinema had been inevitable. Radio and the telephone had made it so. Once the technology was there, it would have to be used. Indeed, Thomas Edison had experimented with synchronizing sound and pictures using his Kinetophone as far back as 1889. At that time the public had not been interested, perhaps feeling that moving pictures were sufficient novelty in themselves to be going on with, but now they responded to cinema's new toy.

Probably the most famous depiction of the early difficulties the sound era afforded Hollywood comes in a hilarious sequence in SINGIN' IN THE RAIN (1952), when cast and director are converting their former silent movie, 'The Duelling Cavalier' into a talkie. The actors must have elocution lessons; the producer trips over a sound cable that was never there before; the harassed director sweats away from the action in his new soundproof booth; and the microphone is concealed either on the actors' clothing, in which case it picks up their heartbeat, or in a bush, in which case it ruins their performance ('I can't make love to a bush!' squeals the actress). There is a lot of permissible comic exaggeration here, but there is also a core of truth. Where to conceal the microphone was a major problem in these early days of sound, largely because it meant all the action had to be grouped around one particular spot and the film became boringly static. To give his film some fluidity the director William Wellman recalled that he attached his mike to a broomstick and just followed the actors around.

Diction coaches were a proliferating breed at this

LEFT: 'You ain't heard nothing yet': Al Jolson in *The Jazz Singer*.

RIGHT: James Cagney impersonates silent horror star, Lon Chaney, in *Man of a Thousand Faces*.

time in Hollywood. However, if silent stars failed when they attempted to cope with sound, very often it was not so much their poor vocal technique as the fact that the way they sounded did not correspond to their screen image. Obviously some foreign actors and actresses had to return to their native film industries because their accents or their English were not adequate for the new situation. Yet Garbo's Swedish-accented English made no difference to her popularity, for her husky melancholy tones seemed an ideal match for the roles she played. On the other hand, Vilma Banky's Hungarian accent gave an exoticism that was quite out of keeping with her ethereal image. In such cases graceful retirement was regarded as preferable to elaborate vocal training. After a disastrous second sound film Norma Talmadge, who was Buster Keaton's sister-in-law and who had made a speciality of playing suffering heroines like CAMILLE (1927), decided to retire with her fortune. When approached by a fan for her autograph, she responded tartly: 'Go away dear – I don't need you any more'.

It obviously took some time for the impact of the transition to sink in. Perhaps the main gain of the coming of sound was the elimination of the cumbersome titles, which had tended to slow down and break up the rhythm of the picture. They had also sometimes put the director at the mercy of the producer, who could substitute titles of his own if the originals were too outspoken. Ingmar Bergman recalls that Victor Sjöstrom told him he was very particular that actors in silent film should speak the words that later appeared in the titles, because he was tired of getting complaints from 'lip-reading, deaf mutes'. The greatest loss was probably the end of the international film and Griffith's idealistic dream of international brotherhood through film. Sound would erect a language barrier. But otherwise much turned on attitude. Chaplin was to remain defiantly silent for ten years. John Ford declared that 'I am a man of the silent cinema, when pictures and not words had to tell the story' and carried that principle triumphantly through his career until his last film in 1966. Similarly with Alfred Hitchcock, who felt that film dialogue was atmosphere more than exposition, and who was to gain some of his subtlest cinematic effects through counterpointing what was

being heard on the screen with what was being seen.

Since the death of the silent movie, there have developed several main ways of recording and celebrating its achievement. One has been mostly unfortunate: the biopic, those showbiz film biographies that generally treat the truth as an irrelevant distraction. Donald O'Connor has played Buster Keaton in THE BUSTER KEATON STORY (1957); Betty Hutton played Pearl White in THE PERILS OF PAULINE (1947); and James Cagney played Hollywood's greatest star of the silent horror film, Lon Chaney, in MAN OF A THOUSAND FACES (1957). None of these can be said to have got near to conveying the subject's greatness, and possibly worst of all has been Rudolph Nureyev as VALENTINO (1977), a film which, he candidly admitted, even sent Ken Russell to sleep – and he directed it. Another development within

this trend has been the recreation of an incident out of silent film history. Not surprisingly, these have been dramatizations of Hollywood's scandals, like James Ivory's THE WILD PARTY (1975) a tentative and rather annoying portrait of a Fatty Arbuckle-type character about to confront his nemesis, and an obscure B-movie THE HOLLYWOOD STORY (1951), which offered a highly implausible solution to the mystery surrounding the murder of director William Desmond Taylor.

An altogether more ingenious and charming conceit was contained in the film GOOD MORNING BABYLON (1986), directed by Paolo and Vittorio Taviani, about two Italians who emigrate to America and become involved with the building of the Babylon sets for INTOLERANCE. Charles Dance was the odd but effective choice for the role of D W Griffith. It was a

LEFT: Two Italian stonemasons work on the Babylon set of *Intolerance* in the Taviani Brothers' film, *Good Morning, Babylon.*

RIGHT: Bernadette Peters as the vamp in Mel Brooks' *Silent Movie.*

film that recreated the ambience of silent film with great affection and splendor. Peter Bogdanovich's NICKELODEON (1976) clearly intended to do the same, since its director is a notorious film buff and since the film closed with the premiere of THE BIRTH OF A NATION, but elsewhere its handling of the comedy was heavy-handed. More expert was Mel Brooks's SILENT MOVIE (1976), which revived the style of silent comedy but within the context of modern movie technology (sound, color etc.). Its only word of dialogue came from the mime, Marcel Marceau, and it included a joke on titles, where a clearly mouthed insult was tastefully transcribed as 'You're a bad boy'. If the film seemed a little inhibited, it was not only because a silent movie from Mel Brooks seemed a contradiction in terms – it was because Brooks so obviously loved the silent film models he was supposed to be satirizing.

With SINGIN' IN THE RAIN, undoubtedly the greatest movie about the silent film era is Billy Wilder's SUNSET BOULEVARD, about a star of the silent era living in seclusion in her rotting mansion and dreaming of a comeback. It was not only Gloria Swanson's magnificent performance that brought back the grandeur and bravura of earlier times. It was also the presence in the film of such veterans as Buster Keaton and H B Warner, and, in particular, the contrasting roles played by two great directors of the silent era, Cecil B De Mille, who plays himself on the set of his latest blockbuster, and Erich von Stro-

heim, who plays a former great director now reduced to the role of butler. Much of Hollywood history was contained in that comparison, as was Wilder's portrait of the harsh new Hollywood that seemed much more cut-throat and competitive than the gleeful improvisations of film in its early days. When Gloria Swanson as Norma Desmond revisits Paramount, De Mille has to tell her that films have changed a lot since her day. She receives a physical reminder of the fact: the feather on her hat is ruffled by a microphone boom, and she pushes the offending mike away as if it were a particularly nasty species of rodent.

What has also happened, as we have seen, has been the representation of silent movies in something approximating their original form. This has meant putting the record straight in two senses: not only showing the film in a manner close to what was originally intended, but being able to reevaluate the film on the basis of much more solid evidence. After the initial excitement of NAPOLEON in its reconstituted form, there is now developing a more agitated discussion about its actual merits, now that the mystification of it as a 'lost' or 'violated' film has been removed. Is it really that well structured, and might one feel that it has Fascist undertones even? One need not necessarily agree with either of those assertions: the point is that the film's restoration has made such discussion at least possible. Similarly, a proper showing of King Vidor's delightful comedy about the film industry, SHOW PEOPLE (1928) might shed a different light on the talents of Marion Davies. To modern film audiences, she was probably best known as the model for the hapless opera singer, Susan Alexander, in Orson Welles's CITIZEN KANE (1941). SHOW PEOPLE demonstrates that she was actually a very accomplished comedy actress.

Recently, Blake Edwards' SUNSET (1988) created an intriguing dramatic situation, not especially well developed, of a real-life Western hero, Wyatt Earp (James Garner) teaming up with a Western star of the screen, Tom Mix (Bruce Willis), to solve a murder. 'The way it really was,' says a caption, 'give or take a lie or two'. It is hard to evaluate the way things were. Historians have said that the cinema has never lived up to the promise of the silent era, but one could equally say the same of drama after Shakespeare. But let this book's final words – as did its first

– go to Gloria Swanson in SUNSET BOULEVARD. 'You're Norma Desmond,' says the pushy young screenwriter (William Holden), recognizing her for the first time. 'You used to be in silent pictures. You used to be big.' Drawing herself up to her full height, Gloria Swanson delivers, as a riposte and with unrestrained relish, one of the great lines of movie history: 'I am big. It's the pictures that got small.'

BELOW: A lot of bottle: Marion Davies in Vidor's Hollywood satire, *Show People*. Davies' career would probably have been more successful had not W R Hearst's forceful campaigns on her behalf alienated the public. RIGHT: A Triumphant return: Gloria Swanson in *Sunset Boulevard*.

BELOW: Based on Somerset
Maugham's melodramatic
story, *Sadie Thompson* has
Gloria Swanson in the title
role as a prostitute who
tries to lure a godly
missionary into wicked
ways on a steamy South
Sea island.

ABOVE: By the end of the
1920s, audiences, ever-
hungry for technological
novelties, succumbed to
the latest cinematic marvel,
the talking picture.

RIGHT: A celebrated vamp,
Theda Bara was a larger-
than-life actress whose off-
screen image was entwined
with the characters she
played. Between 1914 and
1919 she played a variety
of *femmes fatales* in over
40 films.

BUSTER KEATON

IN

SPITE MARRIAGE

Story by Lew Lipton
Adaptation by Ernest S. Pagano
Continuity by Richard Schayer
Directed By

EDWARD SEDGWICK

A **BUSTER KEATON** Production

A Metro-Goldwyn-Mayer PICTURE

LEFT: The second movie Keaton made for MGM, *Spite Marriage* was the story of a tailor's assistant who loved a seemingly unattainable actress. She married him, but only to spite another. Although Keaton had no artistic control over this movie, it still provided an excellent showcase for Keaton's unique comic talents.

LEFT: The cinema's first and probably most famous epic, *The Birth of a Nation* was instantly hailed as a great work of art on its release in 1915. It was also a great financial success, despite the controversy stirred up by its racist bias.

BELOW: Unlike their Western colleagues, post-revolutionary Russian directors tended to make forward-looking films. This constructivist poster is typical of its time.

LEFT & ABOVE: Two posters for De Mille's epic *The Ten Commandments*. De Mille was an excellent story-teller and tried to develop his plots without recourse to sophisticated camera trickery. Unlike the 1956 remake, the silent version consisted of a dual storyline, one half set in 1920s San Francisco, the other in Biblical times.

RIGHT: Douglas Fairbanks lent an amazing energy to this movie, and on its release in 1924 audiences were entranced by the special effects.

LEFT: Seastrom's 1928 masterpiece was an atmospheric drama of mental disintegration. A melodramatic movie, *The Wind* derived much of its power from the penetrating interplay between the characters and the weather.

BELOW: *The Big Parade* was an epic anti-war film that managed to combine impressive spectacle with intense character studies.

NEW BABYLON

THE FAMOUS RUSSIAN FILM OF THE PARIS COMMUNE.

DISTRIBUTED KINO

The BIG PARADE

KING VIDOR'S *production of*
LAURENCE STALLINGS'
Great motion picture story following his stage success with "WHAT PRICE GLORY"

JOHN GILBERT
with RENEE ADOREE

A Metro-Goldwyn-Mayer
PICTURE

MPGP-5478

ABOVE: With music by Shostakovich, *New Babylon*, the story of the Paris commune of 1871 as seen through the eyes of a shopworker, foreshadowed Eisenstein's inventive filming techniques.

LEFT: *The Gold Rush* was Chaplin's finest example of comedy based on complete privation, although he does occasionally overplay the pathos. It is considered by many to be his greatest masterpiece and the culmination of his film art.

ABOVE: Released in 1927, *The General* was one of the high points in Keaton's career. It is a brilliantly conceived story of the Civil War in which the sequence of gags and dramatic action form a brilliant crescendo.

LEFT: A German poster for Eisenstein's classic, *Battleship Potemkin*. It has become a textbook example of creative editing and was twice judged to be the best film ever made. The story was relatively simple and fragmented, but Eisenstein's imaginative treatment has amazed audiences since its release.

BELOW: *October/Ten Days That Shook The World* was designated as an official entry as part of the festivities celebrating the tenth anniversary of the 1917 Revolution. Given full official support, and with the city of Leningrad at his disposal, Eisenstein shot over 150,000 feet of film; just as the first cut was ready, changes in political ideology forced drastic re-editing, much of it under Stalin's personal scrutiny.

Acknowledgments

The publisher would like to thank the following people who helped in the preparation of this book: Ron Callow who designed it; Judith Millidge who edited it; Mandy Little who carried out the picture research; and Pat Coward who compiled the index. Our thanks, also, to the National Film Archive, London who supplied all the illustrations except for the following:

Joel Finler Collection, pages: 2(top right & bottom), 4-5(bottom), 9(top), 10(top & left), 13(top), 14, 16, 17, 18, 21, 24, 32(bottom), 34, 36, 37, 38, 39(both), 40(both), 41, 42, 44-5(all three), 46(top), 48(top), 52, 54, 74(bottom), 75, 76(bottom), 77, 78(top), 79(top), 81, 87, 94, 105(bottom), 106, 107, 110, 113, 115, 125(both), 126(both), 127(both), 128(top), 129(both), 130(bottom), 131(top), 142(bottom), 145, 160(top left), 164(both), 180(left), 181, 184(left), 185, 188(left)

Hulton-Deutsch Collection, pages: 2(top left), 10(right), 59(left), 78(bottom two), 80(top), 82, 83, 85, 86(top), 156, Springer Bettmann Film Archive 109

Museum of Modern Art/Film Stills Archive, pages: 27(both), 29, 30, 57, 60, 65, 112, 118(top), 141, 154, 163(bottom)

Eadweard Muybridge Collection, Kingston-Upon-Thames Museum & Art Gallery, page: 11